THE
BOOK OF
AWESOME
GIRLS

OTHER BOOKS BY BECCA ANDERSON:

THE BOOK OF AWESOME GIRLS

Why the Future Is Female

BECCA ANDERSON

mango
PUBLISHING

CORAL GABLES

Cover Design: Elina Diaz
Cover Photos: (Salty View, spatuletail) / Shutterstock.com
Art Direction: Elina Diaz
Interior Layout: Katia Mena
Interior Photos: (Yaroslav, nerthuz) / stock.adobe.com, (Leonard Zhukovsky, Natata, lev radin, Kathy Hutchins, Jaguar PS, spatuletail, DFree, BAKOUNINE, Joe Seer, Debby Wong, Tinseltown, Salty View, rook76) / Shutterstock.com

For permission requests, please contact the publisher at:
Mango Publishing Group
2850 S Douglas Road, 2nd Floor
Coral Gables, FL 33134 USA
info@mango.bz

For special orders, quantity sales, course adoptions and corporate sales, please email the publisher at sales@mango.bz. For trade and wholesale sales, please contact Ingram Publisher Services at customer.service@ingramcontent.com or +1.800.509.4887.

The Book of Awesome Girls: Why the Future Is Female

Library of Congress Cataloging-in-Publication number: 2021936321
ISBN: (print) 978-1-64250-539-9, (ebook) 978-1-64250-540-5
BISAC category code YAN052060, YOUNG ADULT NONFICTION / Social Science / Sociology

Printed in the United States of America

We are standing on the shoulders of giants: all of the awesome women who came before us and paved the way. This book is dedicated to all the young women and girls who will make it a better world and probably save the planet in the process.

TABLE OF CONTENTS

FOREWORD

Being a woman in today's world can feel like a losing battle. Whether you're watching movies and TV shows or looking at posts on social media, women and girls are bombarded with messages that say they aren't enough. Whether touted as not good enough, smart enough, or strong enough, it seems they simply never measure up. They're also told that they're wrong for being too "this" or too "that"—too outspoken, too aggressive, or too masculine. While women as a whole deal with this societal disapproval daily, women of color—specifically Black women—are at a higher risk of being disadvantaged both personally and professionally as a result. When all you see are signs telling you to change, you're bound to internalize that negativity.

The Book of Awesome Girls serves as a reminder that there is no one-size-fits-all female ideal. As you flip through the pages of this book, you'll come across countless examples of girls and women from all eras of history who made their mark against all odds. Zuriel Oduwole, Greta Thunberg, Dianne Nash, Simone Biles, Payal Jangid, X González, Mary Shelley, Jazz Jennings, Rupi Kaur, Nadya Okamoto, and Darnella Frazier— the individuals highlighted in this book and their accomplishments are nothing short of inspirational! Readers will feel validated seeing a spectrum of backgrounds, personalities, and experiences with which they can identify.

When the world keeps sending you mixed messages, it can be difficult to remember that you are exactly as you should be and all that you bring to the table is valid—your experiences, your hardships, and your successes. *The Book of Awesome Girls* is here to show you that you, too, are awesome, despite the stereotypes that persist in media. Whether you read this book from start to finish or open it up to a random page every day, its positive impact remains the same.

M.J. Fievre

Author of *Badass Black Girl*, *Empowered Black Girl*, and the forthcoming *Resilient Black Girl*

INTRODUCTION

Girls have always been powerful. So much so that millennia of oppression have only made women and girls stronger. In recent years, empowered by social justice movements and social media platforms, girls are now more able than ever to make their greatness known. For example, if a tween girl is really into STEM, she can start her own YouTube channel talking about science and doing experiments and making the world a little bit smarter in the process. And speaking of smarts, girls have a bit of an edge in that their maturation is a little bit more developed.

Rupi Kaur is an excellent example of using social media to create an influential platform. She rose to fame by publishing her powerful poetry to her Instagram and Tumblr, which led her to becoming a bestselling author and overall icon. Another example of extraordinary platform creation is Greta Thunberg who became a phenomenon, piloting a climate neutral boat across the Atlantic Ocean, staging a series of school strikes, and holding all adults accountable for their lack of action. Greta, diagnosed at an early age with Asperger's syndrome, did not let her diagnosis get in her way, and in fact she calls it her superpower and says it enables her to tackle any problem with confidence and drive.

Girls can change the world, and that is exactly what the girls in this book, and many others, have been doing. One of the most poignant examples of a brave young woman's actions is Darnella Frazier, a witness to the killing of George Floyd in Minneapolis, who had the moxie and courage to videotape the horrific 9 minutes and 29 seconds event with her nine-year-old niece in tow. She was threatened but stood her ground and incited global action to fight racial injustice and police brutality.

In this book of awesome girls, you will find world-class athletes, fierce feminists, change-makers, enterprising entrepreneurs, innovative creatives, heroic humanitarians, visionary voices, and world-changing writers. Hopefully these courageous young women will inspire you to empower yourself and the young women in your life and you will ask yourself what you can do to show your awesomeness to the world.

Check out our contest in the back of the book! Post to social media all about the awesome women in your life and you will be entered to win a copy signed by Becca herself!

CHAPTER ONE

AWESOME YOUNG ATHLETES: CHANGING HOW THE GAME IS PLAYED

When someone tells you that you throw or kick like a girl, I have two words for them: *thank you.* To be told that you throw, kick, punch, or play a sport like a girl is the ultimate compliment because it means you are playing as a top athlete. Throughout history, women and girls have dominated the sports world and proved that "playing like a girl" means being tough, determined, skillful, and talented. Women like Serena and Venus Williams, Mia Hamm, Megan Rapinoe, and Lindsey Vonn have set the stage for excellence and have proven to be incredible influences for young women around the world.

Now, those young women and girls are the influencers that have blown people away by their artistry and endurance at such a young age. Own your awesomeness!

CHARLOTTE "LOTTIE" DOD: SHE HAS A LOT(TIE) SPIRIT

Charlotte was the youngest of four children. Just like the rest of her siblings, Charlotte was gifted at sports, especially tennis. By the time Charlotte was eleven years old, she entered her very first tennis tournament at the 1883 Northern Championships in Manchester. Three years later she would earn her first singles title in the West of England Championships and would later earn fifty-five consecutive victories. Not only was Charlotte skilled in tennis, but she also showed expertise in field hockey as well. In fact, she was even a founding member of a women's hockey club in Spital. However, Charlotte did not win an Olympic silver medal in either of these sports. In 1908, she earned her place on the Olympic archery team and won herself a silver medal!

> **"The great joy of games is the hard work entailed in learning them."**
>
> **—Charlotte Dod**

FLORENCE GRIFFITH JOYNER: GO WITH THE "FLO-JO"

Olympian Florence Joyner, widely known as "Flo-Jo," was born in Los Angeles on December 21, 1959. Florence's speed became apparent at the early age of seven, and she did not let it go to waste. She immediately joined the track and field team when she entered high school and served as an anchor on the relay team. Her passion for speed and running continued throughout her college career. Florence finally made her first Olympic appearance at the Los Angeles summer games in 1984. Between her insane speed and dazzling sense of fashion, she stood out as a revolutionary in the sport. Her world records for both the hundred and two hundred meter still stand today, and for that reason she is thought to be the fastest woman in history. Her performance at the Olympics not only won her medals, but many titles as well. *The Associated Press* named her "Female Athlete of the Year," and she was called "Athlete of the Year" by *Track and Field News*. Florence passed away when she was thirty-eight years old due to an epileptic seizure.

> **"When anyone tells me I can't do something…
> I'm just not listening anymore."**
>
> **—Flo-Jo**

WILMA RUDOLPH: "SKEETER"

Wilma Rudolph won three gold medals in track and field in just one Olympics, making her the first ever American woman to do so. However, Wilma did not get onto the podium without encountering her fair share of obstacles along the way. Wilma was born prematurely and extremely sick. Before she could even walk, she had suffered multiple illnesses, including scarlet fever. Her health struggles caused significant weakness in her left leg, and she had to wear a brace for years. However, with great determination she managed her disabilities with physical therapy and was able to run and walk on her own. Growing up during the Civil Rights Era, she went to an all-Black school high school in the South. She was later recruited by track coach Ed Temple to attend Tennessee State University. Her Olympic accomplishments are not only impressive, but, at the time, showed that African Americans and African American women could be successful too. Later, after Wilma retired from the Olympics, she formed the Wilma Rudolph Foundation as a way to promote amateur athletics. She later lost the fight against cancer and passed away on November 12, 1994.

"When I ran, I felt like a butterfly that was free."
—Wilma Rudolph

RUBAB RAZA: LITTLE HUSTLER

Rubab Raza is an amazing young girl who has made the most of her resources and what she got from other people. Rubab started swimming as a little girl in Pakistan. Unfortunately, in Pakistan there is actually a lack of swimming pools and facilities. There is only one swimming pool in the entire country of international quality, and that doesn't necessarily mean it is close to where Rubab lived. So, one could imagine the difficulty to find a place to train in Pakistan. Not only are training facilities lacking, but it is incredibly difficult to get funds for training. The Pakistani Swimming Federation only funded Rubab $30 per month. However, despite the lack of funding and facilities, Rubab still continued to pursue swimming. At the age of thirteen, she became Pakistan's first female Olympic swimmer at the 2004 Summer Olympic games. At the Olympics, she swam the fifty-meter freestyle. Though she was unable to progress in the games, she definitely set a new standard for women in Pakistan, new opportunities for female Pakistani swimmers, and showed girls across the world that no obstacle is unconquerable.

**"I am very happy about my achievement
and consider it a great honor."
—Rubab Raza**

THE FIERCE FIVE: ROLE MODELS FOR THE NEXT GENERATION

Originally known as the Fab Five, this team of gymnasts includes Jordyn Wieber, McKayla Maroney, Gabby Douglass, and Aly Raisman. These five won multiple gold medals in the women's team competition at the London Summer Olympics in 2012. In the competition, they won the US their second team gold medal and the first on international soil.

Gabby Douglas was born in Virginia on December 31, 1995. She is the very first African American to win the Olympic individual all-around title. She took gold at both the 2012 and 2016 Summer Olympics as well. She had her very first experience with gymnastics when she was three years old, when her older sister showed her how to do a cartwheel. Soon after learning the cartwheel, Gaby learned how to do a one-handed cartwheel on her own, and thus her love for gymnastics was born.

> "You've got to be confident when you're competing. You've got to be a beast."
> —Gabby Douglas

McKayla Maroney, or "Mack Air Maroney," is known for her outstanding performance on the vault. She has earned a gold medal with the US Olympic gymnastics team and an individual silver medal for the vault event at the 2012 Summer Olympic Games. The gymnast was ready to go to the 2016 Summer Rio Olympic games, however, due to injuries and health issues, she had to announce her retirement before the games commenced. Growing up in a family heavily involved in sports, she always imagined herself going to the Olympics ever since she was nine years old. McKayla's parents even homeschooled her so that she could train as an elite gymnast. Since retirement, McKayla has pursued acting and has appeared in several TV series such as *The Hart of Dixie*, *Bones*, and *Superstore*.

> **"Looking back isn't going to help you. Moving forward is the thing you have to do."**
> **—McKayla Maroney**

Aly Raisman's love for gymnastics started at an early age. When she was about two years old, her mom enrolled her into mommy and me gymnastics classes. Ever since then, the love to tumble hasn't stopped. Aly started training at an elite level when she was fourteen, and her persistence to train at a young age would further result in many victories. She helped the US gymnastics team grab a win in the 2011 World Championships. Her success continued a year later at the 2012 Summer Olympics in London. As team captain of the "Fierce Five," she won two gold medals and one bronze medal. However, she did not stop there. At the 2016 Summer Olympics in Rio de Janeiro, she also won a gold medal in the women's team competition and silver medals in both individual and team exercises. She is also known for coming forward about the sexual abuse she experienced during her time in the Olympics.

"You have to remember that the hard days are what make you stronger. The bad days make you realize what a good day is. If you never had any bad days, you would never have that sense of accomplishment!"

—Aly Raisman

Kyla Ross, a little kid who was always found at the top of the jungle gym, began her gymnastics career when she was three years old. Kyla's abundance of energy and natural talent has led her to much success. She won a gold medal in the team competition at the 2012 Summer Olympics. She decided to end her Olympic career in 2016 and focus on college gymnastics. Kyla currently attends UCLA and has been on the gymnastics team there since Fall 2016. Since being on the team, she has been named All-American eleven times. On March 16, 2019, she became the eleventh collegiate gymnast to achieve a "Gym Slam," which is earning a perfect ten on all four apparatuses.

> ## "Practice like you have never won. Perform like you have never lost."
> ### —Kyla Ross

Jordyn Wieber says that when she was little her parents noticed she had unusually big muscles, so her parents put her in gymnastics at a very young age, and from there her passion for it never stopped. Since being a part of the Fierce Five, she has retired and is now a head coach for the Arkansas Razorbacks gymnastics team.

SIMONE ARIANNE BILES: SHE MAY BE SMALL, BUT SHE IS MIGHTY

Simone Biles is one of the shortest gymnasts to ever come across the Olympic circuit. Standing tall at a height of four feet, eight inches, one could say that they might have difficulty finding Simone in a large crowd. However, Simone did not let her height become an obstacle. She used her height and body to her advantage and became known for her powerful tumbling in her floor routines. Her dedication and perseverance to push adversity out of the way has earned her the right to be one of the most decorated Olympians in history. Some of her titles consist of the following: 2016 Olympic individual all-around, vault, and floor gold medalist and bronze medalist on the beam, and she won five national championships and four world championships. She also has a trick named after her. It is called the Biles, and it consists of a double flip with legs straightened, ending with a half twist. Not only are Simone's accomplishments amazing, but so is her story. She was born to a mother and father that struggled with drug and alcohol addiction. Since her mother and father were unable to care for her and her siblings, Simone, along with her brothers and sisters, were in and out of foster care. However, despite her difficult childhood, her natural talent for gymnastics could not help but shine.

> **"I'd rather regret the risks that didn't work out than the chances I didn't take at all."**
> **—Simone Biles**

MO'NE DAVIS: BECAUSE I AM A GIRL

Mo'ne Davis has been a champion of girls' sports since she was thirteen, fighting to create more space for young girls and reform students' sports by working to close the gender gap. From a young age she excelled in sports, playing basketball, soccer, and baseball. In 2014, she played in Little League World Series and even pitched a winning game. This made her not only the first African American girl to play in the Little League but also the first *girl* to ever pitch a shutout and earn a win at the Little League World Series. Mo'ne collaborated with M4D3 to create her own line of sneakers and donated some of the proceeds to the "Because I Am a Girl" initiative, which helps raise millions of girls in developing nations out of poverty. She was the youngest athlete to get a feature on the cover of *Sports Illustrated*, and received praise from numerous important public figures, including Michelle Obama.

> **"I just try to be myself. I hope I encourage people just to be themselves, no matter what happens."**
> **—Mo'ne Davis**

YUSRA MARDINI: AMBASSADOR OF HOPE

Yusra was born in Syria, but war chased her from her home—her house was demolished in the Darayya massacre, driving her to flee the country with some of her family members and go to Greece. While she was on the boat, fleeing along with eighteen others, the motor suddenly cut out, and she had to push the boat along with the help of others for over three hours until they arrived at Lesbos. Yusra now lives in Germany. She became a member of the first ever Refugee Olympic Athletes Team and took part in the 2016 Summer Olympics Games in Rio. She is now currently a UNHCR (The Office of the United Nations High Commissioner for Refugees) Goodwill ambassador.

> **"Life will move on. Life will not stop for you because you have pain, no. You have to move on. You have to work on everything."**
>
> **—Yusra Mardini**

MALLORY PUGH: SOCCER'S BLAZING STAR

Mallory Pugh was born in Littleton, Colorado, and started playing soccer at four years old she As a teen, she played club soccer with Real Colorado in the Elite Clubs National League. She then played three seasons with the team at Mountain Vista High School, where she scored forty-seven goals in addition to twenty-three assists. She put off entrance into college and ultimately decided to forgo it to play for the National Women's Soccer League. She has played in the FIFA Women's World Cup as well as the Olympics in Rio, where she became the youngest player to score an Olympic goal for the US.

> "I think it's a really great honor to be playing at the highest level at seventeen... I think it's a once-in-a-lifetime opportunity, and I'm just trying to take it all in."
>
> —Mallory Pugh

CHLOE KIM: THE GIRL WHO SHREDS

Chloe Kim may look like a sweet girl, but she surprises everyone when she shreds up the half-pipe on a snowboard. She started shredding snowboards when she was just four years old and started competing in snowboarding tournaments when she was six years old. Chloe was attending tournaments so often that her father ended up quitting his job so that he could drive her to the mountains every weekend. As of her performance at the 2016 US Snowboarding Grand Prix, she is the first woman to land back-to-back 1080 spins in any snowboarding competition. At the 2018 Winter Olympics when she was just seventeen, she became the youngest woman to win a snowboarding medal. She is said to be the second person to score a perfect one hundred points (the first being Shaun White). Chloe has been featured on the cover of *Sports Illustrated* and has also appeared on the Kellogg's Corn Flakes box, which set a record for "fastest-selling cereal box" in the history of the company.

"I was so fortunate to find my passion and the thing that brought me so much joy at such a young age."

—Chloe Kim

BETHANY HAMILTON: 99 PROBLEMS, BUT ONE ARM AIN'T ONE

Bethany Hamilton is a professional surfer who grew up in Hawaii. At the age of thirteen, Bethany went for a morning surf and almost did not come back. During her surf, she was attacked by a fourteen-foot tiger shark. The shark completely severed her left arm, leading her to lose over 60 percent of her blood and to go into hypovolemic shock. Bethany spent over three months in the hospital recovering before she was allowed to go home. Yet, despite Bethany's extremely traumatic attack in the water and now only having one arm, Bethany still wanted to surf. To do this, she had to adopt a new board with a handle for her right arm and re-learn how to surf. Many were shocked by her perseverance to continue to surf and compete, and it did not go unacknowledged. Bethany earned the ESPY Award for Best Comeback Athlete, the Courage Teen Choice Award, and many others. She has been featured on many TV shows, such as *The Oprah Winfrey Show* and *The Ellen DeGeneres Show*.

"I don't need easy, I just need possible."
—Bethany Hamilton

LAURIE HERNANDEZ: GOLDEN ASPIRATIONS & ABILITY

Laurie Hernandez competed in the 2016 Summer Olympics with the US women's gymnastics team. She won a gold medal in the team competition and a silver for her balance beam routine. Laurie is known best for her artistic routines, the stunning grace she has on the balance beam, and her splendid floor exercises. Laurie was obsessed with the feeling of flying, so it's no wonder her love for gymnastics started early, at the age of six. She also won season 23 of *Dancing with the Stars*.

> **"No matter what race or color you are, you can aspire to do something great."**
> **—Laurie Hernandez**

LILLY KING: SWIMMING'S SPEED QUEEN

Olympian Lilly King's speed in the water definitely makes people wonder if there is really such a thing as a half human, half fish. Some people say that "She swims so fast, you can barely keep an eye on her!" Her lightning speed has enabled her to set the world record for the hundred-meter breaststroke at 1:04.13 seconds! Not only did she set a world record for the hundred-meter breaststroke, but she also won a gold medal in the women's 4 x 100-meter medley relay. Lilly discovered her athleticism in high school when she joined the swim team. Her high school swim team shared its pool with five other teams, and the pool was often crowded with swimmers below her ability. So, to compensate, she got up early in the morning to swim in the pool by herself. Lilly's drive and determination to do well in swimming shows that you can accomplish anything you want to, no matter what the circumstances are.

> **"I am not the sweet little girl.
> That's not who I am."**
> **—Lilly King**

EVGENIA MEDVEDEVA: SHE DOESN'T JUST SKATE, SHE MAKES HISTORY

Evgenia's story is not like most other athletes. She did not originally start figure skating because she was an energetic child or wanted to feel like she was flying; her parents actually put her into the sport at the age of three to improve her figure. Whatever her initial reasoning for starting the sport, Evgenia has proven her skill and mastery by earning more than a few titles. By the time she was seventeen, she had been awarded two Olympic silver medals and was a two-time world, Russian, European, and Grand Prix champion. She also has made several historical records, her first being in 2017 when, at the ISU World Team Trophy event, she became the first female skater to go over the eighty-point mark in the ladies' short program. She is known for her elegance, difficult jumps and transitions, and commonly performing with the Tano variation. She is currently training in Toronto, Canada (as of this writing).

SONJA HENIE: ICE SKATING PRINCESS

Sonja got her first pair of skates when she was six years old, and once she touched the ice she couldn't stop. She loved the cold air against her face as she skated around the ice. It made her feel like she was flying. However, ice skating was not the only sport Sonja showed skill in. Sonja showed talent in skiing and was also a nationally ranked tennis player. Despite her talent and athleticism in other sports, she pursued figure skating and began competing and earning titles when she was just ten years old. As she continued her career in figure skating, her talent followed. By the time she was eleven she participated in her first Olympics and by the time she was fourteen she had already won a gold medal. As a six-time European Champion, a ten-time World Champion, and a three-time Olympic Champion, Sonja has received more titles than any other girl in figure skating. After her career in figure skating, she then turned to the big screen. She began acting and appeared in a series of box office hits, becoming one of the highest paid actresses at the time. Some of her films include *Sun Valley Serenade, Thin Ice,* and *Second Fiddle.*

> **"The world never puts a price on you higher
> than the one you put on yourself."**
> **—Sonja Henie**

SABRINA IONESCU: EQUALITY ON AND OFF THE COURTS

Sabrina is known for changing the way people view women's basketball. Dubbed the "Triple Double Queen," she holds the record in Division I basketball for the most college career triple-doubles (consisting of at least ten points, ten rebounds, and ten assists within a game) with twenty-six, beating out both male and female athletes. She was the 2020 number one pick in the WNBA draft out of the University of Oregon where she was a three-time John R. Wooden national player of the year. She was perhaps molded to be a star at a young age due to her family life. Her parents are Romanian immigrants and taught her to have an unmatched work ethic and to never give up. Having an older brother and a twin brother pushed her to get better in athletics and to overcome adversity. NBA stars such as Stephen Curry, Lebron James, and the late Kobe Bryant endorsed Sabrina as the "GOAT'" and consequently turned the spotlight onto her and women's basketball. Due to her fame, she uses her social media to fight for equality in women's sports and equal pay opportunities. Both on and off the court, she is changing the sports world.

> "My family has always been there for inspiration to keep pushing and one day become a WNBA player."
> —Sabrina Ionescu

HAJRA KHAN: A BALLER ON AND OFF THE FIELD

Born in Sindh, Pakistan, Hajra Khan joined in on the nation's love of soccer. At a young age, she played with her neighbors and hoped for a chance to play on a real team. At age fourteen, she joined a local team, and her soccer career boomed. At only twenty years of age, she became the captain of the Pakistan women's national team and is currently the highest scoring player in its history. She is also the first person on the Pakistan national team to be signed by a foreign club. While it appears that soccer is her passion, her true love may lie in using her success as a platform for action. She uses her social media as a springboard to end the unequal wages female Pakistani players are paid compared to men. She is an ambassador for UNICEF and fights for getting her team affiliated with FIFA. She is currently pursuing a degree in international relations and hopes to fund her own nonprofit aiming to end the stigma surrounding mental illnesses in athletes. While a successful and talented athlete, Hajra demonstrates the ability to use that talent for change.

> **"And we realized that everyone was paid unfairly, treated poorly, and we kind of figured the only way to make this work was to work together for our cause and raise awareness."**
>
> **—Hajra Khan**

NAOMI OSAKA: SHE SPOKE VOLUMES WITHOUT EVEN SAYING A WORD

Naomi Osaka is a tennis legend in the making. At twenty-three years old, this powerhouse of a young woman has won three Grand Slam Singles and is the reigning champion at the US Open. As if those accomplishments did not already make her a household name, her activism makes her even more of an inspiration. Naomi made headlines during the last US Open when she wore face masks displaying the names of several Black individuals who had died at the hands of the police. Without even saying a word, Naomi's actions spoke loudly for who she is and what she stands for.

"Things have to change."
—Naomi Osaka

CHAPTER TWO

TINY PHILANTHROPISTS: YOUNG GIRLS WHO PUT OTHERS FIRST

Some people see a problem and complain. Others, like the girls in this chapter, think, "How can I fix it? How can I make it better?" Kids have a different view of the world. If you ever want to feel better about the world, talk to a young child and they will open your eyes to the good all around you. They have a knack for seeing the world differently and you would be surprised at their ideas to make the world a better place.

When young women and girls are presented with an issue, they have a talent for finding a solution that most adults might not have even thought about. Their inherited kind nature gives them such helpful and unique ideas, and their kind spirits give them the drive to make a difference in the world.

KATIE STAGLIANO: AGE IS NOTHING BUT A NUMBER

Katie Stagliano is the founder of "Katie's Krops," a program initiated after a third grade project in which she grew a forty-pound cabbage in her yard. She donated the cabbage to a nearby soup kitchen and fed hundreds of homeless people in her neighborhood, inspiring her to grow the concept. Currently, the program has expanded to include over one hundred gardens across more than thirty states. These gardens are being maintained by thousands of children—young growers just like Katie.

> **"I have never thought for one moment that I was too young to make a difference, that my actions were limited by my age."**
>
> **—Katie Stagliano**

ALEXANDRA 'ALEX' SCOTT: SWEET AND SELFLESS

Before she had even turned one year old, Alex was diagnosed with a pediatric cancer called neuroblastoma. The doctors told her parents that if she did beat cancer (which was already a low chance), there was even a lower chance of her walking afterwards. However, in just two weeks, at her parents' request to kick, Alex was able to slightly move her legs. Her determination and bravery were helping her beat the odds! When she was four, she decided to set up a lemonade stand to raise donations for childhood cancer research. Her story resonated with people all around the world, and many of them set up lemonade stands of their own to help her raise money. When she passed in 2004 at the age of eight, she had raised $1 million. Her family created the Alex's Lemonade Stand Foundation to honor her legacy.

> **"I'm happy for what I have, not unhappy for what I don't have."**
>
> **—Alexandra Scott**

OLIVIA RIES: OMG, WHAT AN INSPIRATION

Olivia's inspiration to start OneMoreGeneration (OMG) came to her back in 2009 when she and her brother started adopting cheetahs in South Africa to prevent them from going extinct. Olivia, with the help of her brother, then turned her adoption of animals into OneMoreGeneration to encourage animal and environmental conservation. Shortly after Olivia started OMG, the BP Gulf oil spill occurred. She quickly sprang into action and collected animal rescue supplies to personally deliver to the region.

"Do one thing today, that will make a difference tomorrow."
—Olivia Ries

CAPRI EVERITT: THE VOICE HEARD AROUND THE WORLD

Capri began to sing and play the piano when she was just five years old. One day, after practicing, she read a book called *The World Needs Your Kid*. After reading this book, she felt inspired to give back not only to her community but to the whole entire world. Capri wanted to raise funds for abandoned kids by singing national anthems all around the world, and her supportive parents rented their home out and sold their cars to cover the costs of the trip. She ended up singing eighty countries' national anthems in their native languages, and even received a Guinness World Record title for "most national anthems sung in their host countries." After Capri came back from her journey, she and her parents decided to raise even more money and awareness for orphans. They produced a short film called *Anthems: A Journey Around the World*, which won several awards and was a recipient of several international film festival selections.

> **"These days to get noticed and raise money for your cause you have to do something completely crazy, something that nobody's ever done before."**
> **—Capri Everitt**

MELATI AND ISABEL WIJSEN: THE CHANGE WE NEED

These two sisters created their very own company in 2013 called Bye Bye Plastic Bags. They got their inspiration from a country in Africa called Rwanda, where polyethylene bags had been banned some years before, and wanted to enact the same kind of change in their home in Bali, Indonesia. The company started off by encouraging people to say no to using plastic bags. They hosted beach cleanups, staged a hunger strike, and eventually even met with the Bali governor. Melati and Isabel grew their company into a global movement, with teams working in over twenty countries. Their anti-plastic initiative was a huge success and resulted not only in Bali being declared plastic bag free, but in Styrofoam and straws being banned as well.

> "Kids have a boundless energy and a motivation to be the change the world needs."
>
> —Melati and Isabel Wijsen

ADWOA ABOAH: WARRIOR FOR MENTAL HEALTH

Adwoa (which means "born on Monday") signed with Storm Model Management when she was just sixteen years old. However, besides being introduced to fashion at an early age, Adwoa has used her platform to be frank about her battles with bipolar disorder, addiction, depression, and her attempted suicide. Her constant highs and lows inspired her in 2015 to launch a female-focused web hub called *Gurls Talk*. *Gurls Talk*'s mission is to serve as a platform where young girls can openly share their experiences on mental health, body image, and sexuality in a comfortable, trusting, and safe environment. Besides modeling and *Gurls Talk,* in Adwoa's spare time she travels to schools across the globe to speak to young girls about depression and other issues.

"Mental health isn't all of me, but it's a massive part of my journey and a massive part of my whole being."

—Adwoa Aboah

ZURIEL ODUWOLE: STANDING UP FOR WHAT IS RIGHT

Zuriel Oduwole is a Nigerian American filmmaker and education advocate. She traveled to Ghana when she was nine to shoot scenes for a documentary she was creating for a national competition, but while she was there, she was stunned to find that so many of the girls there weren't going to school. Many young girls were selling items on the street, even chasing down cars to sell one item. This inspired Zuriel to start an organization called Dream Up, Speak Up, Stand Up, with the purpose of getting more African girls into schools. Zuriel is considered to be among the most influential, powerful women in the world and has currently met twenty-eight presidents.

"I am unstoppable!"
—Zuriel Oduwole

HANNAH TAYLOR: A LITTLE EMPATHY GOES A LONG WAY

Hannah Taylor is an amazing young girl who has accomplished a lot of success at a very young age. Hannah started her own charity called the Ladybug Foundation when she was about eight years old. Her urge to start this organization came to her one winter day when she saw a man eating out from the trashcan, and she couldn't help but think to herself, "Why? Why? Why?" Since that day, Hannah has dedicated her life to helping the homeless. She has raised over three million dollars through her foundation to fund projects in Canada that give homeless people food, shelter, and safety. Hannah has not only encouraged change through her organization, but also through the written word. She is the published author of *Ruby's Hope,* which is a children's book that inspires hope and caring and empowers young readers to make change.

"Your voice is powerful right now."
—Hannah Taylor

JANINE LICARE AND AISLIN LIVINGSTONE: THE GIRLS WHO ARE SAVING THE RAINFOREST

At nine years old, these two young girls hung ropes in the Costa Rica national park, creating monkey bridges so monkeys can safely cross the roads without having to climb on power lines, which can be deadly. Janine and Aislin started doing papier-mâché when they were about nine years old. They then took their crafts and sold them on the curbside in Costa Rica. They openly admit that their profits were not originally meant to save the rainforests. The two girls would just simply use their earnings to buy food from the deli down the street. However, one day while living in Costa Rica, the girls looked around and were awestruck by the amazing biodiversity the forests contained. Since that day, the girls changed their profits from personal indulgence to saving the rainforest, and thus Kids Saving the Rainforest (KSTR) was born.

"When your backyard is being torn apart in front of your own eyes, anyone would be compelled to try and save it."
—Janine Licare

ANNIE WIGNALL: THE LITTLE GIRL WHO CARES A LOT

Annie Wignall knew that giving back was what she wanted to do ever since she was eleven years old. Her idea for the Care Bag Foundation originally came to her when her mom came home from work one day asking Annie to start collecting essentials (shampoos, soaps, etc.) because her mom's work was doing a donation drive. However, after Annie collected for the drive, she didn't want to stop.

> **"Thanks to the help of my incredible mom, countless volunteers, distributors, and supporters, Care Bags has grown bigger and better than I ever dreamed possible."**
> **—Annie Wignall**

MACKENZIE BEARUP: CHANGING THE WORLD ONE BOOK AT A TIME

Mackenzie is a young girl who many adults should strive to be like. Mackenzie was diagnosed with a disorder called complex regional pain. Dealing with chronic pain constantly, she often turned to books to help keep her mind off the physical and emotional pain. She didn't want other kids to suffer with pain as she had in the past, so she created Sheltering Books when she was just fifteen. Sheltering Books is a nonprofit organization that collects and donates books to homeless shelters and hospitals. Her nonprofit also helps develop reading spaces, such as libraries and reading rooms, where these books can be kept, used, and read. Mackenzie is an incredible young girl because she never let her disability prevent her from doing the things she wanted to accomplish in life or let stereotypes define her abilities and potential. Instead, she turned her disability into her inspiration.

"When I read, it's a real escape."
—Mackenzie Bearup

SAVANNA KARMUE: THE HEART TO MAKE A DIFFERENCE

Savanna Karmue began her crusade to promote heart health at six years old, after visiting her Sunday School teacher prior to a heart procedure. She knew then that she wanted to be a cardiologist and began YouTubing advice on keeping a healthy heart. On her eighth birthday, she started her own nonprofit; the following year, she transferred that knowledge into a book called *Happy Heart Advices: Introduction to Your Heart, Vol. 1*. Her passion did not stop there, and she began speaking at local churches and seminars and eventually became a keynote speaker at several high-profile symposiums. Savannah's curiosity led her to dig deeper, and she found that childhood obesity is a root cause of heart problems. In 2016 she launched the Happy Heart Challenge, which educates and provides resources to children on living a healthy lifestyle. Savannah is ambitious and has set a goal to cut childhood obesity in half by 2031. With her work ethic and drive, Savannah will continue to inspire others to have a "happy heart."

> **"...I didn't want to wait to become a cardiologist to help people, and I wanted to start immediately."**
> **—Savanna Karmue**

CHAPTER THREE

CIVIL RIGHTS SHAKERS: CHANGING SOCIETY ONE DAY AT A TIME

The right to vote and other vital civil rights came about as a result of unstintingly hard work and action by many people—many of whom we will not know the names of, but we have to thank. The story of the civil rights movement is emblazoned with the names of many heroes, including Fannie Lou Hamer, Rosa Parks, Congressman John Lewis, W.E.B. Du Bois, Martin Luther King Jr., Medgar Evers, and Malcom X. It has been wonderful to see daughters of Martin Luther King Jr., Yolanda and Bernice King, and daughter of Malcolm X, Ilyasah Shabazz, carry on this important work. However, some of the bravest individuals and strongest voices belong to the young women who marched, sang, and protested until laws were changed and justice was served.

Some of these girls, being so young, may not have even known they were fighting against racism or discrimination and probably did not understand the magnitude of their courageous actions. These young girls simply knew what was right and what was wrong, and even at a young age they knew what it meant to be on the right side of history. Many young girls today continue to emulate their actions in the continued fight for equality.

CLAUDETTE COLVIN: TAKING A STAND BY TAKING A SEAT

Several months prior to the arrest of Rosa Parks, Montgomery-born Claudette Colvin, a fifteen-year-old high school student, refused to give up her own seat on a segregated bus on a ride home from school and was arrested. She would later become one of four female plaintiffs in *Browder v. Gayle*, a supreme court case that resulted in the desegregation of busses in Montgomery and Alabama.

> **"I knew then and I know now, when it comes to justice, there is no easy way to get it."**
> **—Claudette Colvin**

DIANE NASH: A LEADER FOR FREEDOM

Diane was born in 1938 and raised in Chicago, Illinois by her parents Leon and Dorothy Nash. After she finished high school in Chicago, she went to attend Howard University in Washington, DC. After one year, she transferred to Fisk University in Nashville, Tennessee. While Diane was living in Nashville, she was exposed to the Jim Crow Laws and their effects on the lives of Black people for the first time. The unfair treatment angered her and made her heart wrench, so Diane decided to join the civil rights movement, and this moved her to start several campaigns. Some of her campaigns included the integration of lunch counters in Nashville, the Freedom Riders, and the desegregation of interstate travel. She helped facilitate several voting rights initiatives, including the Alabama Voting Rights Project and the Selma Voting Rights Movement—both of which helped lead to the passage of the Voting Rights Act of 1965 in congress.

> **"Freedom, by definition, is people realizing that they are their own leaders."**
>
> **—Diane Nash**

SYLVIA MENDEZ: BRAVE BEYOND WORDS

Sylvia Mendez played a key role in the 1946 desegregation case *Mendez v. Westminster*. The case was instrumental in the civil rights movement and blazed a trail for integration in the future, allowing Latinx students to attend "whites only" schools and not just the segregated "Mexican" schools. Following the desegregation, Mendez (a young girl of Mexican and Puerto Rican heritage) later became one of the first Latinx children to go to a formerly all-white school. She grew up to become a prominent activist for civil rights.

"It's about everybody coming together. If you start fighting for justice, then people of all ethnicities will become involved."

—Sylvia Mendez

RUBY BRIDGES: THE LITTLE GIRL WHO MADE HUGE HISTORY

The 1954 *Brown v. Board of Education* case concluded about three and a half months before Ruby was born. The court's decision made it unconstitutional to separate schools for Black and white kids. However, it was not until 1960 that the court ruling was finally put into practice. Ruby was the first Black student at William Frantz Elementary School in New Orleans. Ruby had to be escorted by federal marshals every day on her way to school, in the face of violent protests. Once Ruby started attending the school, many white parents transferred their kids to different schools and many teachers refused to teach Ruby. Ruby later became an iconic figure in the civil rights movement and is featured as the subject of a famous Norman Rockwell painting, *The Problem We All Live With*.

> "Don't follow the path. Go where there is no path and begin the trail. When you start a new trail equipped with courage, strength, and conviction, the only thing that can stop you is you!"
>
> —Ruby Bridges

GEORGIA GILMORE: MAKING HISTORY HAPPEN

Georgia grew up in Montgomery, Alabama during the time of the Civil Rights Era—a time when Black people were only seen for the color of their skin. Every day when Georgia took the bus to work, she was forced to sit in the back. She eventually grew tired of paying money and financially supporting a discriminatory system. This eventually inspired her to join the Montgomery Bus Boycott. However, finding alternate means of transportation for everyone in town cost money. Thankfully, Georgia was an amazing cook! So, during the boycott meetings Georgia would sell food to help fund with the repairs that needed to be made and vehicles that needed to be purchased. Georgia was the girl behind the scenes and helped make the Montgomery Bus Boycott happen!

> **"We felt that we had accomplished something that no one ever thought would ever happen in the city of Montgomery."**
> **—Georgia Gilmore**

AUDREY FAYE HENDRICKS: NINE YEARS OLD AND STRONGER THAN MOST

Audrey was a brave and confident young girl who wasn't going to let the color of her skin hold her back. In 1963, nine-year-old Audrey left school and joined the Children's Crusade. Held in Birmingham, Alabama, the Children's Crusade was a peaceful demonstration in which thousands of youths contested segregation. Thousands of students, including Audrey herself, were arrested during the march. She was thrown in the Juvenile Hall for about a week, making her one of the youngest civil rights demonstrators to be jailed during the movement. The violent actions taken by law enforcement gaining international attention on a large scale, as photographs taken during the Children's Crusade incensed viewers all over the world.

"It was no way for me not to really be involved, my parents were involved from the point that I could remember..."

—Audrey Faye Hendricks

DAISY BATES: SPEAKING FOR THE SILENCED

Daisy grew up in a small sawmill town of Arkansas called Huttig in a shotgun house with her biological mother and father. In a horrible turn of events, her mother was raped and murdered by three local white men, and the case was never solved due to lack of devotion to the case. After her mother's death, Bates was then handed off to be raised by family friends and she never saw her biological father. As one could imagine, the death of her mother and the events that followed impacted her for life, even though they occurred early in her childhood. Because Daisy had to confront the existence of racism very early in life, it drove her to become a lifelong activist.

> "No man or woman who tries to pursue an ideal
> in his or her own way is without enemies."
>
> —Daisy Bates

CHAPTER FOUR

ACTIVISTS: YOUNG CRUSADERS OF REFORM

It may surprise you how easily activism comes to young people. Children and teens have this beautiful way of seeing the world as it could be and the most determined of them take the steps to actually get the world to that beautiful place. Even when circumstances were not in their favor, these brave kids knew what they had to do. Indigenous Americans have a way of thinking seven generations ahead of themselves, which is not a practice taken up by the majority of adults today. Kids, however, have a similar way of looking at the future—a way that makes it better for everyone.

The heroic young women in this chapter stood up and spoke out even when they were the only ones doing so, and inspired not only their fellow young people, but also adults who were blown away by their strength. The young women took on issues such as feminism, LGBTQ+ rights, school safety/gun reform, climate change, unequal education, and racism and did not let anything, including their age, get in the way of them making a difference.

THANDIWE CHAMA: A LEADER FOR ALL

Thandiwe Chama is a Zambian educational rights activist, who got her start when her school closed down due to a lack of teachers. Though she was only eight years old at the time, Thandiwe helped lead her classmates in the search for a new school, and she has persisted in her activism ever since. At sixteen years old, she was awarded the International Children's Peace Prize for her efforts to help more and more children gain access to education. She also advocates for the rights of African individuals living with AIDS and HIV. Through her activism, she has gained international recognition and has brought more awareness to these diseases as well as to educational issues in her home country.

> **"...I love knowing my rights and my responsibility as a child."**
>
> **—Thandiwe Chama**

HANNAH CAMILLERI: PROTECTING AND SUPPORTING GIRLS ALL OVER THE WORLD

Hannah Camilleri found her activism after posting about being sexually harassed at a gig. She quickly found many responses from other girls who had experienced similar harassment at these events and sprang into action. Hannah and her friends founded Girls Against in 2015 to open up the discussion between fans, bands, and organizers to put an end to harassment at gigs. Since its inception, Girls Against has gotten support from bands, been featured in publications, and continue their blog covering feminist ideas and the music world.

> **"Because we're all teenagers, we understand and fear the same things [the people messaging us] do."**
>
> **—Hannah Camilleri**

HEBH JAMAL: STANDING UP AND WALKING OUT

Hebh Jamal is a young leader in the fight against Islamophobia. In a post 9/11 world, she is trying to change the image and rhetoric that surrounds Muslims in America. In 2017, the Trump administration announced the "Muslim ban," essentially banning US entry to travelers coming from seven different countries consisting of majority Muslim populations. Hebh spoke out against this travel ban and organized a citywide walkout that involved thousands of local high school students. These students left their classes to protest Donald Trump's election and fight bigotry. Since Trump's ban, Hebh has continued to organize protests, rallies, and be a strong progressive voice in the resistance against Trump's anti-Muslim rhetoric.

> **"We are called "kids" when we use our voice
> to enact change, but we're not kids..."**
>
> **—Hebh Jamal**

AHED TAMIMI: DEFENDING HER HOME AND LEADING A GENERATION

Ahed Tamimi's life has been full of protesting and fighting for the rights of her people almost from the start. Growing up in Israeli-occupied Palestine, she has witnessed harassment and violence against her people at the hands of occupying forces her entire life. Starting out when she was just eleven years old, Ahed was making headlines through her protests and resistances against Israeli soldiers for arresting members of her family. In 2017 her fame soared after a protest she was a part of turned violent. Protesters were throwing stones at soldiers, and soldiers entered her family home. Ahed ended up slapping and otherwise fighting soldiers in a video that quickly went viral. She was arrested and served time, earning her high school degree behind bars. Ahed hopes to move forward studying law to help further protect her people in this time of unrest.

> **"...I always say I am a freedom fighter. So I will not be the victim."**
>
> **—Ahed Tamimi**

LILY MADIGAN: A CHAMPION FOR TRANS RIGHTS

Nineteen-year-old Lily Madigan made her mark in British politics when she became the first transgender teenager to hold a position in the Labour Party. The party faced some backlash, with many people arguing that a trans woman—especially a teenager—shouldn't be allowed the role of officer. Lily had gained some attention for her queer activism prior to this, after taking her school to court for demanding that she wear boys' clothes, denying her use of female restrooms, and refusing to use her chosen name. She won her case and received an apology from the school, and has continued to stay strong even when confronted with copious amounts of online transphobia. She fights for trans rights and hopes to one day become the first transgender member of Parliament—until then, she is continuing to make history in other ways.

> **"Your words have the power to hurt, to heal, to inspire, or discourage. Remember that."**
> **—Lily Madigan**

AMIKA GEORGE: HELPING GIRLS IN NEED. PERIOD.

Amika felt inspired after reading about Freedom4Girls, a charity that usually provides menstrual products to young students living in Kenya but had to forward products to Leeds (a city in the United Kingdom) because there were girls that could not afford them. Amika founded the campaign Free Periods and gathered over 200,000 signatures on an online petition. When she was seventeen, she organized a peaceful protest in which around 2,000 people dressed up in red to demand government action. The goal of the protest was to get free menstrual products for those in the free meal programs in schools. Amika also aims to dismiss the idea that periods are shameful.

> "In a patriarchal society, periods are seen as a secret because a big percentage of the people in power aren't faced with them every month. When I think about a world that has gender equality, it's one where periods are openly discussed."
>
> —Amika George

ZHAN HAITE: EMPRESS OF EDUCATION

Zhan Haite is an educational activist in China. She bravely stood up for what she believed in despite objections from her parents and a government with a poor track record of accepting civilian criticism. She challenged the Chinese government's practice of refusing migrant workers the opportunity to take their high school entrance exams. Thousands of students were denied the chance to improve their lives and ease the adversities wrought on them by poor economic situations. Even though the odds were stacked against her, her efforts did not go in vain—the government took steps to loosen some of the regulations that discriminated against these migrant workers.

> **"My idols are Martin Luther King and Aung San Suu Kyi. Both paid a heavy price in the pursuit of equality, freedom, and democracy."**
>
> **—Zhan Haite**

JULIA BLUHM: YOUNG FEMINIST WITH A BIG VOICE

As part of the body positivity movement, Julia Bluhm is altering the ways bodies are shown in popular media. She is changing the beauty landscape one magazine at a time—when she was fourteen, she petitioned the editor-in-chief of the popular *Seventeen* magazine to feature more realistic models in their issues. Because of her candor, they eliminated photoshopping and began displaying authentic, healthy bodies. Julia continues her body image activism as a blogger, encouraging other young girls to hold brands accountable on body inclusivity.

> "...teenagers offer a lot. A lot of times, people think of teenagers as not caring, and that's a big mistake."
> —Julia Bluhm

MARY GRACE HENRY: A SMALL STEP TO HUGE CHANGE

Mary is a young seamstress who decided to use her passion as an opportunity to enact positive change in the world. She created and sold reversible headbands at her school's bookstore, with the intention of donating all of the profits to underprivileged girls. She wanted to improve the lives of these girls by helping them finance their education, and she has been extremely successful in doing so. What started as a small school project has bloomed into Reverse the Course, a charity that has sold thousands of hairpieces and sent over one hundred girls to school in countries like Uganda, Haiti, and Paraguay.

> **"When you see a need, act. Dream big but start small taking little steps."**
> **—Mary Grace Henry**

CASSANDRA LIN: FEEL THE HEAT

In fifth grade, Cassandra Lin learned that many people in her town could not afford heat. She also discovered that cooking oil could serve as biofuel. With this new knowledge, she reach out to local restaurants and asked them to donate their leftover cooking oil to her so she could recycle it. As her initiative grew into Project Turn Grease Into Fuel (or TGIF), Cassandra started to move outside her community and collect from restaurants in other nearby areas. Every gallon of grease the program receives is turned into biodiesel to help economically stressed families.

**"Youth voice is the key to securing
the future of our planet."
—Cassandra Lin**

ANOYARA KHATUN: SAVING CHILDREN, CHANGING THE WORLD

Anoyara comes from a family of little means in West Bengal. When she was just five years old, she also lost her father. When she turned twelve, her family's financial circumstances compelled her mother to listen to the advice of a distant relative, who suggested sending her to a family who could take care of her and give her an education. However, Anoyara and her mother had been deceived—she became a victim of child trafficking and was forced to work as domestic help in Delhi instead. There, she was abused, kept in terrible conditions, and unable to contact her family until she was rescued by the organization Save the Children. When she returned home and saw how many children were suffering that same way, she became an avid children's rights activist. She has fought against exploitation and child marriage, and has helped rescue hundreds more children. Her efforts led to her becoming one of the youngest recipients of the Nari Shakti Award.

> **"Children will have wings, won't be afraid of anything and are able to reach to the skies."**
> **—Anoyara Khatun**

X GONZÁLEZ: THE VOICE WHO SPOKE UP

After the mass school shooting at Marjory Stoneman Douglas High School in 2018, students rose to the occasion to advocate for gun control, especially outspoken senior X González, a survivor who delivered a powerful speech during a rally that gained national attention. They played a key role in organizing the March for Our Lives and have continued the fight to implement stricter gun laws, having since co-founded the gun control advocacy committee Never Again MSD.

> **"We are going to be the kids that you read about in textbooks."**
>
> **—X González**

VICTORIA PANNELL: WALKED OUT SO OTHERS DON'T HAVE TO RUN

Victoria is a seventeen-year-old activist from Harlem, New York. At sixteen, she organized the #NationalSchoolWalkout to protest gun violence in schools. On Friday, April 20th, 2018, Victoria inspired hundreds of thousands of students in every state in America to walk out of their classrooms. After her protest, Victoria became the youngest person to sit on Manhattan's Community Board. She also started another nonprofit called Tools for Change, an organization that facilitates youth success by offering such services as mental health counseling and strategies for money management. Victoria also has a history of protesting child sex trafficking, even giving a TED Talk on the subject in 2016 at a San Diego TEDxYouth event.

> **"People think it's an 'over there' issue, and it's not, it's happening right here in the United States."**
>
> **—Victoria Pannell**

GRETA THUNBERG: LET'S HELP HER SAVE THE PLANET

Greta Thunberg, a young girl from Sweden, has received international acclaim for her powerful climate change activism. At fifteen, she began speaking out on the importance of immediate action to slow climate change when, using school time to protest outside the Swedish Parliament. She and other students organized a movement called Fridays for Future, which involved organized school climate strikes. She has demanded that the government take steps to reduce carbon emissions, in line with the Paris Climate Agreement, and gave a speech at the 2019 UN Climate Action Summit that initiated her rise to fame. She has been featured in *Forbes* and *TIME Magazine,* and has inspired over 20,000 students in over 270 cities to hold climate strikes as well.

"I don't want your hope. I don't want you to be hopeful. I want you to panic... to act as if our house is on fire."

—Greta Thunberg

SONITA ALIZADEH: SINGING TO SAVE LIVES

Sonita is an Afghan activist against forced and child marriages. As a child, Sonita was almost married twice—once when she was ten years old, and again when she was sixteen. To gain attention about forced marriages, she released a video called "Brides for Sale." This was a huge risk—she was living in Iran at the time, where, by law, women are not allowed to sing in public. Despite this, her song became a viral hit, and she received a scholarship that gave her the opportunity to study in the United States. She continues to perform music and inspire young women to stop conforming to restrictive, outdated traditions.

> **"Everyone is important—both world leaders and everyday people. I hope that together we can create the biggest campaign in the world to end child marriage."**
>
> **—Sonita Alizadeh**

YARA SHAHIDI: USING HER PLATFORM FOR GOOD

In 2014, Yara Shahidi landed the role of Zoey Johnson on the TV show *Black-ish*. She has since then used her platform to encourage young people to become more politically involved. She started an organization called We Vote Next (formerly Eighteen x 18) that encourages young adult voter registration and increased voter turnout. She also started a digital meet up platform for high schoolers to discuss self-improvement and higher education.

> "I don't think I'd be doing the work I'm doing if I wasn't constantly inspired by the other young people doing this work, by the other young people doing work I didn't even realize had to be done. I feel like we constantly educate one another."
>
> —Yara Shahidi

BANA AL-ABED: LITTLE ADVOCATE, HUGE INSPIRATION

If you give a seven-year-old a phone, they'll most likely going to play Candy Crush. Bana, however, utilized the power of Twitter to raise awareness about the effects of the ongoing Syrian Civil War. In 2016, with the help of her mother, she tweeted a series of posts from Aleppo that documented the harrowing sieging of the city. Those tweets broke the hearts of people around the world. Now twelve years old, Bana continues to advocate for her fellow Syrians and uses her platform to draw global awareness to the horrors taking place in her homeland.

"You must do something for the children of Syria because they are like your children and deserve peace like you."

—Bana al-Abed

JAZZ JENNINGS: ALL THAT JAZZ

At just six years old, Jazz Jennings was featured in a television special on trans children and interviewed by Barbara Walters. This led to even more subsequent high profile public appearances. As a young adult, she has used her influence as a YouTube personality and spokesperson to continue to educate the public on trans issues and advocate for LGBTQ+ rights. She has her own reality TV series, *I Am Jazz*, has taken on a few acting roles, and has also become a published author.

> "If I wasn't confident in who I am or didn't like
> the fact that I was transgender, then I would
> not I have gotten as far as I have today."
>
> —Jazz Jennings

MALALA YOUSAFZAI: THE DEFINITION OF STRENGTH AND ENDURANCE

Malala is an astounding young girl who has been through more than one can imagine at her age. Her hometown of Swat Valley, once a popular tourist destination, was seized by the Taliban in 2008. They provoked fear in the community and banned girls from being educated, so many were afraid of sending their children to school. However, Malala would not back down or let the Taliban stop her or any other girl from receiving their education. She began to openly speak for human rights and women's education. However, the Taliban eventually saw Malala as a threat to their campaign. One day, when Malala was fifteen years old, a masked gunman boarded her bus and shot her in the side of the head, nearly killing her. Malala's continuous human rights efforts have made her the youngest person to receive the Nobel Peace Prize.

"If one man can destroy everything, why can't one girl change it?"
—Malala Yousafzai

SOPHIE SCHOLL: STOOD UP FOR HER BELIEFS, NO MATTER THE COST

Sophie Scholl was a German student and political activist who studied at the University of Munich during World War II. She spread anti-war leaflets at the university with the help of her brother as part of the White Rose, an organization that encouraged peaceful resistance against the Nazi regime. She was eventually caught and questioned by the Gestapo, but she dutifully protected the identities of other White Rose members. She was found guilty of treason and was executed by guillotine in 1943. Her courage in putting her life on the line to resist the Nazis left a huge impact, and her memory will continue to be honored for years to come.

> "I am, now as before, of the opinion that I did the best that I could do for my nation."
>
> —Sophie Scholl

MARLEY DIAS: THE MAIN CHARACTER

At thirteen years old, Marley Dias founded a campaign called #1000BlackGirlBooks. Accustomed to only ever reading books about white boys, she initiated this book drive as a way to highlight literature about Black girls. The goal was to gather 1,000 books featuring protagonists who were Black girls and then donate them to girls at other schools. She ended up collecting more than 9,000 in just a few months! She says, "I'm working to create a space where it feels easy to include and imagine Black girls and make Black girls like me the main characters of our lives." She also has released a book of her very own called *Marley Dias Gets it Done: And So Can You!*

> "I believe activism is the true source of change in the world. Pushing to change social structures in communities that you are a part of is critical for making real lasting change."
> —Marley Dias

EDNA CHAVEZ: USING HER VOICE

Edna Chavez is a gun reform activist from Los Angeles. At the March for Our Lives rally in Washington, DC, she gave a stirring speech about the normalization of gun violence in our society. Having lost many of her own friends and family to gun violence in South LA, she addressed how students of all ages are taught in class how to protect themselves from shooters. Since then, she has spoken at other prominent events in an effort to educate people on the realities of gun violence and inspire young voters to make a difference. "For decades, my community of South Los Angeles has become accustomed to this violence," she told the crowd. "It is normal to see candles, it is normal to see posters, it is normal to see balloons, it is normal to see flowers honoring the lives of Black and brown youth who have lost their lives to a bullet."

> "Remember my name. Remember these faces.
> Remember us and how we are making change.
> La lucha sigue [the fight continues]."
> —Edna Chavez

ELYSE FOX: FIGHTING TO END THE STIGMA

Elyse Fox is a filmmaker and mental health awareness advocate. She founded the Sad Girls Club, a platform dedicated to educating young women on mental health issues and increasing awareness. Her documentary, *Conversations with Friends,* details her own personal struggles with mental illness. She continues to find ways to open up healthy discourse around the subject and strives to create a culture in which these conversations are no longer considered off-limits.

"I can live a full, fruitful life with mental health issues."
—Elyse Fox

NADYA OKAMOTO: STANDING UP FOR MENSTRUAL EQUITY

Nadya Okamoto, a young entrepreneur born in New York City, founded an organization called PERIOD alongside her friend, Vincent Forand. The nonprofit provides menstrual products such as pads and tampons to communities in need, as well as supports an end to the tampon tax. It promotes worldwide menstrual equality, seeking positive change on both a legal and social level.

"I felt like I had something new to offer the world and a duty to speak up. I felt empowered."
—Nadya Okamoto

CHAPTER FIVE

DEFINING HISTORY: GIRLS WHO LEAVE THEIR MARK

It is true that well-behaved women seldom make history. It is also true for awesome girls who are willing to take a stand. History is full of powerful visionaries and strong leaders changing the world for the better with a unique invention, a startling astronomy discovery, or just an extraordinarily lived life. By now, it should not surprise you that a large amount of those visionaries and leaders were young women and girls who, by just being themselves, literally made history.

These young women made their way into our history books by following their hearts and their instincts and never accepting the idea, "that's just the way it is." By being authentically themselves, their names have gone down in history and their legacies have inspired, and will continue to inspire, generations of spunky, fierce girls following in their footsteps.

ANNE FRANK: THE NAZIS DIDN'T SILENCE HER

Anne Frank was a Jewish girl who was born in Germany. When the Nazis seized control of the country, she and her family moved to the Netherlands to evade the Gestapo. Their hiding place was unfortunately uncovered eventually, and she and her family were arrested. Anne died in a concentration camp when she was just fifteen years old. The sole surviving family member, her father Otto, was moved reading her diary, which she received as a birthday present, after the war and published it posthumously. Her diary recounting the events was published and continues to echo the effects of the Holocaust as it has been published in more than sixty languages.

"How wonderful it is that nobody need wait a single moment before starting to improve the world."

—Anne Frank

HELEN KELLER: A SYMBOL OF STRENGTH AND PERSEVERANCE

At nineteen months, Hellen Keller was diagnosed as both blind and deaf. The story of how Helen's teacher, Anne Sullivan, rigorously taught her how to communicate is widely known. Helen was highly political, lobbying for the women's suffrage movement, standing for labor rights and socialism, and opposing military intervention. In her travels, she brought hope to many individuals with similar disabilities and motivated real change in the world, as more opportunities and resources were provided for people who were visually impaired. She was an active member of the Industrial Workers of the World, as well as of the Socialist Party of America.

"The best and most beautiful things in the world cannot be seen or even touched—they must be felt with the heart."

—Helen Keller

MAYA LIN: ART THAT SPEAKS

At twenty-one, Maya Lin won an anonymous competition to create a war memorial. After she was announced the winner, many took issue with Maya being of Asian descent and with the design of her memorial. Maya had to appear before Congress to defend her right to create and her design choice. Her creation, the Vietnam War Monument in Washington, DC, now memorializes the names of hundreds of soldiers.

> **"I try to give people a different way of looking at their surroundings. That's art to me."**
> **—Maya Lin**

VENETIA PHAIR: KICKING BUTT AND TAKING NAMES

How many kids can claim they named a planet? Venetia Phair is credited with naming Pluto in 1930, when she was just eleven and the then-ninth planet was newly discovered. Phair had told her grandfather that the planet should be named after the Roman god of the Underworld, and he alerted a friend who happened to be an astronomy professor at Oxford University, *TIME* previously reported.

> **"...I said, 'Why not call it Pluto?' And the whole thing stemmed from that."**
> **—Venetia Phair**

JOAN OF ARC: STANDING TALL FOR HER BELIEFS

Joan of Arc was a peasant girl in the early fifteenth century France—a time of constant war, as they battled England for control of the French throne. As a young woman, Joan was known to be very spiritual, and she believed that the saints guided her life. When she one day heard their voices entreating her to fight on behalf of France, Joan herself took part in the war effort and quickly proved to be a valuable asset in battle against the British. It was during the siege of Orleans that she first became known as hero—after conveying her visions to the Dauphin Charles, she was allowed to take part in the fight and even led her own force of soldiers. Her prominent role in lifting the siege led to her being well respected throughout the country. When she was about nineteen years old, she was captured and martyred by the British. In the year 1920, she was canonized as one of France's patron saints.

"One life is all we have, and we live it as we believe in living it. But to sacrifice what you are and to live without belief, that is a fate more terrible than dying."

—Joan of Arc

SHAMMA BINT SUHAIL FARIS AL MAZRUI: A YOUNG WOMAN OF GREAT ACCOMPLISHMENTS

At just twenty-two years old, Shamma was appointed to the role of the United Arab Emirates' Minister of State for Youth Affairs. She is the youngest person in the world to hold the title of government minister. In this position, Shamma hopes to help young people get more involved in society and government affairs, and to make it more accessible to do so.

> **"Hopelessness results when youth are not seen as resources, and apathy results when they're not seen as assets."**
>
> **—Shamma bint Suhail Faris Al Mazrui**

ARTEMISIA GENTILESCHI: TURNING PAIN INTO ART

Artemisia Gentileschi was a trailblazer for female artists. She was born in 1593, which was a time where women were not necessarily welcomed with open arms in guilds or artistic academies. Her father was a celebrated painter, and she certainly followed in his footsteps. She was supported by the famous Medici duke, Cosimo II, and was the first woman to gain acceptance into the Florentine Academy of Fine Arts. Most famously, at age eighteen, Artemisia was assaulted by her teacher for refusing to marry him. In court, she testified against him despite that not being the norm. This branded her with the reputation of being a "promiscuous" woman, yet she did not let that affect her career. Instead, she took that pain and turned it to her art. She painted historical and biblical paintings, which was rare for a woman at the time. From this fresh perspective, she was able to portray the servant Judith as a heroine in her paintings. It is said that her paintings double as an autobiography. When applying that lens to her art, you can see that Judith doubles as a war cry to all other oppressed women. Her work is now getting known, after being hidden under the name of her father. Artemisia demonstrated willpower and determination at such a young age to become a pioneer of women's art.

PAYAL JANGID: THE RIGHT TO A SAFE EDUCATION

Payal is from a village in an area of India called Rajasthan. Due to widespread poverty, Rajasthan's conditions are difficult for young children to navigate—many girls as young as twelve years old are forced into marriage and lose access to education. As a preteen, she herself escaped a child marriage and eventually went on to become an activist for children's rights. She leads the Bal Panchayat (Children's Parliament) in her village, which addresses a lot of the issues children are faced with in schools and in their home lives. She fights to protect girls from marriage, support their right to go to school, and helps make her village a more child-friendly place.

"Life is a beautiful mess of uncertain things."
—Payal Jangid

SOPHIE CRUZ: FOR HER FAMILY

When Sophie was just five years old, she wrote a letter to Pope Francis asking him to help prevent her parents from being deported out of the US. Her parents are undocumented immigrants from Mexico, and Sophie wanted to help them and others who were just like them. During the pope's visit to Washington, DC, Sophie dodged his security detail to deliver her letter to him. Though caught, Pope Francis motioned for Sophie to approach him, and the security personnel acquiesced, allowing her to meet him and give him the letter she had poured her heart into. Ever since, Sophie has continued to fight for the rights of immigrants, even giving a speech at the DC Women's March when she was just six years old. She said, "Let us fight with love, faith, and courage so that our families will not be destroyed."

> "I have the right to protection. I have the right to live with my parents. I have the right to live without fear. I have the right to be happy."
>
> —Sophie Cruz

MARGARET KNIGHT: INVENTOR AND INSPIRATION

The inventor of the flat-bottomed paper bag started her inventing career at just twelve years old. In 1850, it was unheard of for women to have intellectual property or have a science driven career. However, Margaret had an inquisitive mind and was always thinking of solutions. After visiting her brothers at a cotton mill, she created a safety device that swept the industry. The device helped keep shuttles from falling out of the powered textile looms and hitting workers, something she had observed during her visit. Eighteen years later, she invented a machine that would manufacture the flat-bottomed paper bag we still use today. She fought for her patent rights against a man who tried to steal her ideas from her and succeeded. Her numerous inventions and patents show that women can have a field in ingenuity too.

**"I'm only sorry I couldn't have had
as good a chance as a boy."
—Margaret Knight**

AMANDA GORMAN: THE HILL SHE CLIMBED

Amanda Gorman is the definition of a history maker. Growing up in Westchester, CA, as the daughter of a middle school teacher, Gorman found a passion for writing and spoken words starting at a young age. This passion would lead to Gorman becoming the youth poet laureate of Los Angeles at only sixteen years old and then at nineteen, only three years later, she would become the first national youth poet laureate. Amanda was inspired by Malala Yousafzai's moving 2013 speech at the United Nations and continues to gain inspiration from powerful women such as Oprah Winfrey and Michelle Obama. Using this inspiration, Amanda continued to write her beautiful poetry through her young adult life and caught the attention of First Lady Jill Biden, who arranged for Gorman to speak at the 2020 inauguration, making her the youngest writer to ever recite a poem at a presidential inauguration. This was particularly special because much like President Joe Biden, Gorman struggled for years with a speech impediment but used that struggle to work even harder and that is what makes her the brilliant young woman she is. Amanda also has a twin sister, Gabrielle, who is also an activist as well as a filmmaker. If Amanda's life wasn't exciting enough, she just signed a modeling deal!

> **"But I don't look at my disability as a weakness.
> It's made me the performer that I am and
> the storyteller that I strive to be"**
>
> **—Amanda Gorman**

CHAPTER SIX

LITTLE ENTREPRENEURS: GIRLS WITH VISION

You think homework is hard? Try starting your own business. The young women discussed in this chapter simultaneously did both—some while they were still in elementary school! These girls created clothing lines, energy companies, and food empires at incredibly young ages, setting a wonderful example not only for their peers but for adults as well.

The incredible thing about these young women is that none of their businesses were purely for profit. Each business either solved a difficult problem or created a solution for someone, or something, in need. These girls were not out to build companies just for the sake of building companies; these girls set out to help those in need using their extraordinary creativity and intelligence.

ALLYSON AHLSTROM: A FIERCE PHILANTHROPIST

Allyson Ahlstrom is young philanthropist who started her own charity as a young teen. The company, called Threads for Teens, is a clothing drive that provides new clothes to girls living in foster homes, group homes, and situations of poverty who would otherwise be unable to afford them. What started off as a small service project grew into a full-time boutique, as Allyson aspires to inspire young girls and provide them with self-esteem and confidence by expanding their shopping options. With the support of some influential individuals like Queen Latifah, Allyson was even able to take Threads for Teens on a national tour, visiting over forty cities and outfitting thousands of girls across the country.

> **"When I started out, I had no idea I'd get to where I am now."**
>
> **—Allyson Ahlstrom**

MAYA PENN: ECO-FRIENDLY FASHIONISTA

Maya is a young entrepreneur who was born and raised in Atlanta. In 2008, at the age of eight, she started Maya's Ideas, her own eco-friendly fashion house. She partners with major brands to help them address sustainability and find ways to make fashion more friendly for the environment, promoting the development of eco-consciousness in the industry. She has also done three TED Talks that have gone viral and was chosen as Oprah's youngest SuperSoul100 entrepreneur.

"Be creative, be curious, and watch as your awesomeness is unleashed."
—Maya Penn

MIKAILA ULMER: QUEEN BEE

At four years old, Mikaila Ulmer learned about bees' importance in the environment and decided that she wanted to do something to protect them. She entered a local business competition for children in the area with her family's homemade lemonade recipe, sweetening the lemonade with locally produced honey. Mikaila donated a portion of sales toward conservation organizations working to prevent the extinction of honeybees. She has sold her "Me & the Bees" lemonade at events and went on *Shark Tank* to grow the business. She was even able to secure a partnership with Whole Foods!

> **"Don't be discouraged by life's little stings, get back up and spread your wings!"**
> **—Mikaila Ulmer**

ANN MAKOSINSKI: LIGHTING THE WAY FOR OTHERS

Ann Makosinski is a Canadian inventor and public speaker. When she was fifteen, she participated in the 2013 Google Science Fair. Her entry was flashlight of her own invention, powered completely by body heat! This discovery served two purposes: it reduced the waste produced by flashlight batteries, and it offered an affordable light source to people who didn't have the means to pay for electricity. This invention was followed by another—the eDrink mug, which converts the excess heat from beverages into energy that can be used to charge a phone. She presented her eDrink on Jimmy Fallon's *Tonight Show* and has won a number of awards and investments from climate organizations. She has also forged major brand partnerships, as well as been featured in *TIME Magazine* and *Forbes'* 30 Under 30 list.

"If I don't do something constructive every day, I feel like I have wasted my time, and I almost feel guilty for not doing something I could have learned from."
—Ann Makosinski

STEPH GABRIEL: PLASTIC, BUT MAKE IT FASHION

Steph Gabriel is an activist, entrepreneur, and marine scientist. She founded Ocean Zen in 2014, a company borne of concern for the environment and the marine life being harmed by the copious amounts of plastic that make their way into our oceans. The company sells sustainable swimwear that is made from materials recovered from the ocean, including recycled plastic bottles and abandoned fishing nets. Steph is "saving the ocean, one bikini at a time," as the company slogan goes.

"Don't waste another second wondering if and how. Just launch straight into your passion and go for gold."
—Steph Gabriel

GITANJALI RAO: LITTLE SCIENTIST, BIG INVENTION

When Gitanjali was just eleven years old, she learned about the water crisis in Flint, Michigan and was motivated to make change. She invented Tethys, a device that detects the presence of lead in water. Tethys is based on carbon nanotubes that can send information via Bluetooth. She entered Tethys into the 2017 Discovery Education 3M Young Scientist Challenge and was awarded $25,000. Gitanjali has faith that the device may be even more accurate than the test options currently available. Because the prototype cost only slightly more than $20 to put together, her invention would also be more accessible due to its affordability. Her She was selected by Gizmodo as one of the most heroic earthlings, earned the title of America's Top Young Scientist, and was awarded among many other distinctions.

> **"I was always someone who wanted to put a smile on someone's face. That was my everyday goal, just to make someone happy."**
>
> **—Gitanjali Rao**

HANNAH GRACE: BEAUTIFULLY YOU

After her father challenged her to make the same beauty products found in stores, ten-year-old Hannah Grace created a line of bath products using natural ingredients. Her line BeYOUtiful stems from the idea that beauty comes from within. She believes that her brand showcases that you do not have to be anyone but yourself in order to be beautiful. While being a successful young entrepreneur is truly awesome, what makes her even more special is her heart. She was diagnosed with Type 1 Diabetes and celiac disease and wants to help others who experience those diseases too. Twenty percent of all purchases from BeYOUtiful go toward JDRF and Beyond Type 1, organizations that are actively striving to increase awareness about and fund research for Type 1 Diabetes.

Quote: "You don't have to be like a model or anyone else to be beautiful, you just have to be you."

—Hannah Grace

ASIA NEWSON: A SHINING LIGHT IN THE BUSINESS WORLD

"Detroit's Youngest Entrepreneur" started her own candle business modeled after her father's sales career. Her company blew up, and after several years, she is still creating and selling candles. Her business has since grown into Super Business Girl, a workshop-based mentorship program. The company, of which she is co-founder and CEO, gives back to children just like her so that they can learn how to become entrepreneurs too. From the proceeds of the sales, Asia buys her school supplies and purchases food and clothing for less fortunate kids.

> "You can't give up because you're a child. And you can't be afraid to fail. That's one thing that I've learned."
>
> —Asia Newson

CHAPTER SEVEN

BEAUTIFUL ROYALS: GIRLS WHO RULE THE WORLD

Who *rules* the world? *Girls*—literally. Throughout history, some of the bravest and most competent rulers have been women and large portions of those women were brought to power at very young ages. Despite their ages, these young women stepped up and led entire nations at ages where *our* biggest problem was passing geometry.

These girls led with elegance and poise while being burdened with making the hardest decisions one could ever have to make, but by doing so, they made history and proved that girls do, in fact, rule. These powerful girls led people all over the world from China to Georgia, India to Egypt, and were responsible for entire nations of people at very young ages. The girls in this chapter not only showed up and did their job day in and day out, but actually made the world a better place by simply being awesome.

MARY, QUEEN OF SCOTS: RULING BEFORE LEARNING TO CRAWL

As King James V's only surviving child with a legitimate claim to the throne of Scotland, Mary ascended to throne when she was still an infant. In fact, she was only days old when the King passed away. Regents ruled Scotland in her place while she grew up in France, where she eventually became queen consort. In her life, she wore the crowns of four different nations: Scotland, France, Ireland, and England.

> **"To be kind to all, to like many and love a few, to be needed and wanted by those we love, is certainly the nearest we can come to happiness."**
>
> **—Mary, Queen of Scots**

ST. JADWIGA OF POLAND, ALSO KNOWN AS HEDWIG: IT TAKES A QUEEN TO BE A KING

Jadwiga took the throne of Poland when she was just ten years old after her father Louis the Great, King of Hungary and Poland passed away. Jadwiga was actually named "king" of Poland at the time to emphasize the separation of the Polish and the Hungarian kingdoms. For the next two years, she was the sole ruler of the region, and then she was pressured to marry Jogaila of Lithuania by Polish government and influential business members. To enable the marriage, Jogaila was willing to be christened and promised to unite his country with Poland and to enforce Christianity in Lithuania. From what it seems, Jadwiga seemed unhappy in her marriage with the older man and spent most of her time caring for the poor and sick. She also founded several monasteries. On June 22, 1399, when she was only twenty years old, she gave birth to her only child who survived for just three weeks. Jadwiga then followed her child five days later. In 1997, she was canonized by Pope John Paul II.

> **"[Jadwiga was] the real-life princess who was one of Poland's holiest and greatest rulers."**
> **—Virginia Durkin O'Shea**

CHRISTINA OF SWEDEN: WITH GRACE AND DIGNITY

The daughter of Sweden's King Gustavus Adolphus and his wife Maria Eleonora, Christina was their lone surviving child. She took the Swedish throne when she was just six years old, after her father died in battle, but officially began her rule when she was eighteen. She is remembered for her scholarship—Christina's education was highly extensive at the time, and even more so for a woman. She studied art, philosophy, and languages, as well as ballet to improve her grace and poise, and is considered to be among the most learned women of her century.

> **"We should never believe anything we have not dared to doubt."**
>
> **—Christina, Queen of Sweden**

CLEOPATRA OF EGYPT: A LEGEND IF THERE EVER WAS ONE

Cleopatra, a highly educated woman mastering Greek, Latin, and Egyptian, is most widely known for her exotic beauty and her romantic liaisons and military alliances with Julius Caesar and Mark Antony. The throne was passed on to her when she was just eighteen years old after her father's passing. During her reign, she built up the Egyptian economy by establishing trade with many Arabian nations. This resulted in the people of Egypt being incredibly fond of her.

"I will not be triumphed over."
—Cleopatra

NEFERTITI OF EGYPT: THE PHARAOH'S EQUAL

Nefertiti became queen of Egypt when she was fifteen years old. Imagine, instead of sitting in a high school biology class, you are ruling a nation! It definitely sounds like more fun than learning about meiosis and mitosis, doesn't it? Anyway, Nefertiti ruled Egypt alongside her husband, and because of their close relationship she was able to acquire more and more religious and political power than any other queen before her. Nefertiti's relationship was unique for her time because not only did her husband see her as an equal but so did the Egyptian people. In many artistic depictions, Nefertiti is shown wearing the attire reserved only for a pharaoh, as well as being the same height and size as her husband.

TAMAR OF GEORGIA: PROVING THEM WRONG

Tamar was the only female monarch in the history of the nation of Georgia. The Georgian throne revolved entirely around a patriarchal system, leading Tamar to be called "King Tamar." However, Tamar broke patriarchy when she was just eighteen years old and was given sole reign of the throne after her father died around 1184. Since Georgia had previously never had a female ruler, many were hesitant and doubtful about Tamar's ability to govern Georgia and reacted against her policies. However, Tamar proved to her people that despite her gender and lack of experience she was a powerful and capable ruler. Under Tamar's rule, Georgia successfully defended itself against its enemies. The Kingdom of Georgia was threatened by invasion from several Muslim rulers and Tamar was able to help lead the Georgian army to victory. Tamar also launched several military campaigns to extend the borders of Georgia and funded many cultural and arts projects such as works of literature and monuments.

"One knows a lion by its claws and Tamar by her actions."
—Unknown

MEERABAI: LIVING THROUGH LOVE

Meerabai was an Indian princess born in 1498 who loved to sing, dance, write poetry, and was heavily devoted to her husband and to the Hindu deity, Krishna. She sometimes would even refer to her husband as Lord. Her husband passed away shortly after they got married, but instead of participating in the "widow's rite" of burning along with him on his pyre, she took on a life of religious fervor. Meerabai would frequently dance and sing with commoners in the street, but actions were heavily looked down upon by her family and were seen as "unfeminine" behavior according to the Indian culture. Her family even tried to have her killed several times because they were so embarrassed of her actions. Luckily, Meerabai survived all assassination attempts. Meerabai shows us that wealth, titles, and materialistic objects are not the most important things to life. She also inspires us to always follow our passions, because passion is what makes life worth living.

"Don't forget love: it will bring you all the madness you need to unfurl yourself across the universe."
—Meerabai

PRINCESS PINGYANG OF CHINA: THE REAL-LIFE MULAN

Pingyang was the real-life Mulan that every little girl dreams of being. It is uncertain if the story of Pingyang is treated more as a legend or actually based off a historical person, but I thought her story was worth mentioning. It is said that Pingyang's father, Gaozu, was a rebel leader who fought against the Sui dynasty. Pingyang and her husband had needed to escape, because her father had been imprisoned before for leading a rebellion. Her father told her that it would be easier for to hide since she was a woman. While she was hiding, Pingyang shared her wealth with a group of peasants and then later turned them into warriors. The small group of warrior peasants would later join up with other armies to create a force consisting of over 70,000 soldiers. Along with "The Army of the Lady," as they were known, Pingyang and her father waged war against the army of the Sui—and defeated them. Pingyang's military brilliance allowed her father to seize power from the Sui dynasty and take the throne, eventually becoming emperor of the Tang dynasty.

"As you know the Princess mustered an army that helped us defeat the Sui Dynasty...the princess personally beat the drums and rose in righteous rebellion to help me establish the dynasty...She was no ordinary woman."

—Emperor Gaozu

AMEERAH AL-TAWEEL: A PRINCESS WITH A HUMANITARIAN HEART

After interviewing Saudi Arabia's prince Alwaleed Bin Talal for her school paper, eighteen-year-old Ameerah Al-Taweel stole his heart. Though she was no royal, the two instantly clicked and were married in 2008. Her marriage earned her the title of princess, as well a life of wealth and prosperity—but instead of taking it easy, she chose to use her newfound privilege to help others. She has fought for women's rights in Middle Eastern countries, gotten involved in numerous humanitarian charities, and engaged in extensive philanthropy. She has remained on good terms with Alwaleed since their divorce and continues to do great work to help make the world a better place.

> **"Throw yourself to the edge that you're always scared of. Try being independent; do it your way. You'll love it."**
>
> **—Ameerah Al-Taweel**

PRINCESS ALEXANDRA OF HANOVER: SKATING TO THE THRONE

Alexandra is the only child of Princess Caroline of Monaco and Prince Ernst August of the defunct (no longer existing) kingdom of Hanover. She is thirteenth in line for the Monégasque throne, and was also in the line of succession to the throne of Britain until her confirmation in the Catholic Church. Besides being a princess, Alexandra is also an Olympic ice skater. When she was ten years old, she was given a pair of ice skates for Christmas, marking the start of her skating career. She competed for the first time in Toulon, France, at the age of eleven, and when she was twelve, she was awarded the cup of the Monégasque Federation of Skating.

> ### "You can just call me Alex."
> ### —Alexandra of Hanover

OTHER NOTABLE ROYALS:

- **Princess Charlotte of England**

- **Princess Estelle, Duchess of Östergötland**
  At the age of nine, she is currently second in line for the Swedish throne after her mother.

- **Princess Catharina Amalia**
  Currently age seventeen, she will someday succeed her father as Queen of Netherlands.

CHAPTER EIGHT

AMAZING WRITERS: FIGHTING BATTLES WITH WORDS

Your pen is mightier than any sword. Words can make an enormous difference—they can inspire, they can empower, and they can make change. Writers have the power to open our eyes and move us to tears. It takes a special person to be able to simply put pen to paper and inspire a whole generation. Often, that person is a young woman who can wow the world with only her words.

These young women have written stories that have stood the test of time and have continued to resonate with audiences decades after publication. Their creatively and unique perspectives may be surprising coming from such young women but that is all the more reason to continue lifting up the young women in our lives. You, your sister, or your best friend could be the next voice of your generation—you just need to pick up a pen.

MARY SHELLEY: MOTHER OF SCI-FI

Mary was born on August 30th, 1797, in London, England. She didn't have a formal education, but her father did have an extensive library, so Mary would often grab a book and sit to read by her mother's grave. Besides reading she also said that she would be caught daydreaming often trying to escape from her challenging home life. In 1807 she published her first poem, "Mounseer Nongtongpaw." Mary Shelley wrote *Frankenstein,* which is considered to be the first science fiction novel, when she was eighteen. Not long after she wrote *Frankenstein,* she married and had two kids. However, her marriage did not get much easier than her childhood—it was riddled with adultery, financial struggle, and the loss of both children. Shelley wrote several additional books, including *Valperga* and *The Last Man,* before she died of brain cancer in London when she was fifty three years old. Mary's life is awe-inspiring because even in a life full of hardship she still managed to create beautiful novels that not only have lasted for centuries but have also inspired others to create as well.

"Beware; For I am fearless, and therefore powerful."
—Mary Shelley

JANE AUSTEN: IN HER OWN WORDS

Jane was born on December 16, 1775, in Steventon, Hampshire, England. She grew up in quite a large family—she was her parents' seventh child—so one could imagine that the learning environment was somewhat compact. Throughout their childhood, Jane and her siblings read in their father's library and wrote and performed plays. As she got older, she started writing in notebooks, and by the time she was a teenager she already crafting her first novel, *Love and Friendship*. This novel, which consisted of love letters, parodied the romantic fiction genre. However, she wrote anonymously because, at the time, it was extremely difficult for women to get published. During her young adulthood, Jane spent her time helping her family with the household, playing the piano, socializing with neighbors, and attending church. Unfortunately, Jane fell ill with Addison's disease when she was forty-one. She continued to write for a few years, but as her health deteriorated, she stopped writing and then died on July 18, 1817. Her brother Henry was the one who ultimately revealed Jane as the author of her anonymously published works, and he played a role in their continued distribution after her death.

"It isn't what we say or think that defines but what we do."
—Jane Austen

DOROTHY STRAIGHT: A VIVID IMAGINATION

In 1962, Dorothy's mother asked her a question: "Who made the world?" Dorothy responded with her own picture book, which she created over the course of one evening. Her parents thought her response to the question was marvelous, so they sent it to Pantheon Books. Patheon Books loved Dorothy's response as well and decided to publish it. She's the youngest commercially published female author for her book *How the World Began* that she released at the age of four.

> **"The importance children place on the familiar and the furniture of their surroundings comes through in Dorothy's words and pictures."**
>
> **—Kirkus Reviews on Dorothy's book**

AMARIYANNA (A.K.A. "MARI") COPENY: LITTLE MISS FLINT

Amariyanna, or Mari, of Flint, Michigan, wrote a letter to President Obama in early 2016. The eight-year-old wanted to meet him along with a few other officials when she and her family paid a visit to Washington, DC, for the congressional hearings on the water crisis that was happening in their hometown. Obama replied to her letter and traveled to Flint, saying he wanted to see the problem for himself and help to work on a solution. Since then, Mari has continued to be known as an activist, doing everything she can to help improve life in her community.

> **"You don't have to have a huge following or a ton of money to help in your community. You can start small, you can help an elderly neighbor take out their trash or read to the smaller kids in your neighborhood."**
>
> **—Mari Copeny**

SAMANTHA SMITH: A GIRL LOOKING FOR ANSWERS

Samantha Smith grew up in Maine during the Cold War. She is known for penning a letter to Yuri Andropov, the CPSU General Secretary at the time, in which she asked why tensions between the Soviet Union and the US were so high. Yuri Andropov replied to her letter personally and invited her to visit the Soviet Union. She accepted, and her visit received widespread international attention. She was recognized as a Goodwill Ambassador and was quoted saying that she thought the Russians weren't any different than "us." She also participated in peacemaking activities as an ambassador to Japan, and went on to become a child actress. She passed away in a plane crash at thirteen.

"If we could be friends just by getting to know each other better, then what are our countries really arguing about?"
—Samantha Smith

VIRGINIA WOOLF: BRILLIANCE UNBOUND

One of the most prominent modernist authors of the twentieth century, Virginia Woolf was born into a family of means in London. She was an innovator, whose nonlinear and stream-of-consciousness-style narratives made her a literary pioneer. Her life was marked by loss, with her mother passing in 1895 and her stepsister following shortly after. This continuous sense of loss sparked a serious mental breakdown, which became a pattern in her life. Her father encouraged to start her writing career, but not long after, he too died, and Woolf had another mental breakdown. Between 1910 and 1915, Virginia's mental health was precarious. However, she did not let it get the best of her, because during this time she published her first novel, *The Voyage Out.* Some of her other well-known works include *A Room of One's Own*, *Mrs. Dalloway*, *Orlando,* and *To the Lighthouse.*

> **"I am made and remade continually. Different people draw different words from me."**
> **—Virginia Woolf**

HYPATIA OF ALEXANDRIA: A GENTLEWOMAN AND A SCHOLAR

Not only was Hypatia a writer and one of few women in Greek academia, she was also a polymath who lived in the Eastern Roman Empire. She studied philosophy, mathematics, and astronomy, and wrote a commentary on Diophantus's *Arithmetica*. It is believed that she also edited the text we have today of Ptolemy's *Almagest*. Though a lot of her writings and teachings were controversial at the time, many people were listening to her thoughts and ideas and were captivated by her perspective. Records indicate that Hypatia was well loved, and she became a martyr among philosophers after her shocking murder at the hands of a mob.

"Reserve your right to think, for even to think wrongly is better than not to think at all."

—Hypatia of Alexandria

SYLVIA PLATH: PRECOCIOUS POET

Sylvia Plath's literary career started earlier than most. At the age of eight, Sylvia was already writing poetry. Even at a young age, people took note of Sylvia's skill. One of her poems that she wrote as a child was later published in the *Boston Herald's* children section. Over the next few years, Sylvia never let go of her pen and ideas and continued to write and get published in several regional magazines and newspapers. When she entered college, she kept pursuing her talent by studying English literature. However, while at college, Sylvia suffered from serious depression that almost resulted in her taking her own life with her mother's sleeping pills. After six months in a psychiatric facility, Plath later returned to college to finish her degree. Plath has become one of America's greatest young authors, and she is credited with advancing the genre of confessional poetry and is best known for her two books *The Bell Jar* and *Ariel.*

"The worst enemy to creativity is self-doubt."
—Sylvia Plath

VERONICA FRANCO: A POET FOR ALL WOMEN

Veronica Franco was born in Venice in the 1500s. She was her family's only daughter and received private tutoring as a child along with her brothers. She spent much of her adult life tending to her children and managing a household of servants and tutors. She became a consort of high standing in order to support herself and her household, and eventually got involved with a reputable Venetian literary salon, which was run by adviser Domenico Venier. She frequented the salon, where she built connections with male poets and even wrote her own poetry. Her first collection of poetry was published in 1575, and it serves as a reflection of her experiences as a courtesan. Today, she is considered to be a feminist advocate, and her work critiqued some of the traditional portrayals of women in literature during her time.

> **"When we too are armed and trained, we can convince men that we have hands, feet, and a heart like yours."**
> **—Veronica Franco**

RUPI KAUR: AN OLD SOUL WITH A FRESH TAKE ON LIFE

Viral poet Rupi Kaur got her start on Instagram, where she would post photographs of her poetry for her online audience. In 2015 she published *milk and honey*, a collection of poetry and prose that was incredibly successful on the book market. It is primarily about survival, and highlights themes related to femininity, heartbreak, love, and sexual trauma. Rupi has made headlines for her activism and condemnation of the taboos surrounding menstruation. Many attribute a recent revival in poetry sales to her work, and it is clear that she has played a pivotal role in getting a whole generation of young people interested in the craft of poetry.

> **"We grew up in a time with every single one of our moves being recorded and documented forever and in that was this idea that we can't make mistakes, but when that's not happening, you're also not growing."**
>
> **—Rupi Kaur**

CHAPTER NINE

IN THE SPOTLIGHT: LUMINARIES SHARING THEIR LIGHT

They say that intense pressure is what makes diamonds. These young women are perfect examples of the result of pressure. The pressure of being in the spotlight can weigh on people tremendously. The pressures of the entertainment industry can be very difficult, especially since one's every move is on display. The young women in this chapter prove that even when the spotlight is shined down on them, they use their platforms for good.

These awesome girls spread positivity and bring awareness to causes such as the environment, equality, and the right to an education, while breaking barriers and shattering stereotypes. They show that their greatest talent of all is kindness, humanity, and generosity of spirit. Let's shine that spotlight on them!

BINDI IRWIN: CREATING HER OWN LEGACY

Since her father Steve Irwin's tragic death in 2006, Bindi has carried on his legacy and become a well-known conservationist, actress, and television personality. She hosted her own television show, *Bindi the Jungle Girl*, when she was just nine years old. The show was a nature documentary with the purpose of teaching kids about all different kinds of animals and getting them interested in protecting those animals. She has released songs, starred in movies, and continues to take a stand for wildlife conservation.

> "Every time you lose an animal, it's like losing a brick from the house. Pretty soon the house just falls down, you know?"
>
> —Bindi Irwin

MILLIE BOBBY BROWN: A MOVER AND A SHAKER

Millie Bobby Brown is the youngest person ever to feature on *TIME's* "100 Most Influential People." After her quick rise to fame for her lead role on Netflix's *Stranger Things* (for which she earned a Primetime Emmy Award nomination when she was just thirteen), she became UNICEF's youngest Goodwill Ambassador. She continues to use her platform for good, encouraging her fans to sign petitions and fight for children's rights around the world.

"As long as I give my best, and I know I'm centered and know what I'm doing, then that's all that matters."

—Millie Bobby Brown

GRACE VANDERWAAL: DREAM BIG

This little girl is an absolute wonder! Her music career began back home in Suffern, New York, by doing open mic nights and posting covers online and on YouTube. However, she stole the hearts of many as she strummed her ukulele and sung her heart out on the stage of *America's Got Talent*. As she played her original song "I Don't Know My Name" on stage at the age of twelve, she never knew how much her life would change after that moment. After her performance on *America's Got Talent,* she released her first full-length album in November 2017 called *Just the Beginning.* Since the release of her album Grace has won various awards, such as the Radio Disney Music Award for Best New Artist, Teen Choice Award, and the youngest person to ever be included in Forbes's 30 Under 30 Music List. Grace shows us that we should never quit on our dreams no matter what they might be.

"I am not like everyone else. I don't pretend to be. I don't want to be. I am me."

—Grace VanderWaal

BILLIE EILISH: THEREFORE SHE IS

Billie Eilish began her love of singing and writing music early on in her life. Today, at only nineteen years old, Billie Eilish is a household name. She has gained recognition for her incredible music around the globe and has been nominated for (and won!) many prestigious music awards. Most notably, Billie's hit song "Bad Guy" won Grammy Awards for both record and song of the year.

"I'm gonna make what I want to make, and other people are gonna like what they're gonna like. It doesn't really matter."
—Billie Eilish

ADUT AKECH: BEAUTIFUL INSIDE AND OUT

Modeling superstar Adut Akech was born in South Sudan before eventually moving with her mother and siblings to Australia as refugees at the age of six. She was scouted multiple times at a young age but did not become a model until she was sixteen years old. She has been on the cover of *Vogue* several times, including the coveted September issue. In 2019, Adut was named "Model of the Year" at the British Fashion Awards.

"Before I'm anything else, I am a refugee, and I'm so proud of that."

—Adut Akech

TAYLOR SWIFT: COUNTRY STAR TURNED POP SENSATION

Taylor Swift is one of America's most famous singers and songwriters. However, before all the glam and fame, she spent her childhood in Reading, Pennsylvania as a simple girl singing at county fairs and local events. Yet, the simple life did not fit a girl with such a big voice. Her parents quickly recognized their daughter's talent and moved to Nashville, Tennessee to help pursue her music career. After an amazing performance at the Bluebird Café in Nashville when she was fourteen, she landed her first record deal with Borchetta's Big Records. Soon after her record deal, she released her single "Tim McGraw," and it quickly became a chart-topping country music hit. The single also appeared on her debut album, which sold around five million copies. At the time of writing, she has nine successful albums and has won many awards, including Grammy Awards for Best Album and Best Video, the Billboard Music Award for Woman of the Year, and so many more.

> **"Words can break someone into a million of pieces, but they can also put them back together. I hope you use yours for good."**
> **—Taylor Swift**

ROWAN BLANCHARD: GIRL MEETS WORLD (AND MAKES IT A BETTER PLACE)

Rowan Blanchard played the character of Riley Matthews on *Girl Meets World*, a Disney Channel show that acted as a sequel to the '90s classic *Boy Meets World*. While that role is what she is most well-known for, it is her youth activism and essays on intersectional feminism that have put her over the edge. At just thirteen years old, the actress spoke at the UN Women US National Annual Conference about gender equality. Also, in January of 2015, she addressed a crowd of 75,000 people at the Women's March in Los Angeles. Rowan said, "I believe in the effable power of community. If women, if queer people, if people of color have survived this long in a world that refuses to represent them, that must amount to a force much greater than one man with nothing more to invest in but his ego."

> **"People used to always talk down to me, like, 'Oh, you're so young,' but now I recognize that my age is an advantage; there's a lot more I can do."**
>
> **—Rowan Blanchard**

MARIA TALLCHIEF: DANCED HER WAY INTO OUR HEARTS

Maria Tallchief, an indigenous woman from the Osage nation in Oklahoma, was both the first major prima ballerina in America was well as the first Native American woman to ever hold the prima ballerina title. She was considered a revolutionary in the dance world and was a major star amongst American ballerinas. She held the title of prima ballerina at the New York City Ballet for eighteen years and performed with the Paris Opera Ballet. She received many awards for her contributions to the arts.

> "Dance from your heart and love your music,
> and the audience will love you in return."
> —Maria Tallchief

YUAN YUAN TAN: GRACEFUL ON AND OFF THE STAGE

Yuan Yuan Tan is currently prima ballerina at the San Francisco Ballet and guest principal dancer at the Hong Kong Ballet. She started dancing when she was eleven and had great success in dance competitions around the world. Her accomplishments granted her celebrity status, and she has been celebrated in many high-profile magazines, including *Vogue China*. She has even been called "the greatest Chinese ballerina of all time." She has received brand endorsements from numerous influential brands and is considered a fashion icon.

> **"Inspiration comes when you let go."**
> **—Yuan yuan Tan**

MISTY COPELAND: TAKING CENTER STAGE

Misty Copeland is the first African American woman to become a principal dancer for the American Ballet Theatre. She began learning ballet when she was thirteen, which is usually considered a bit late. Her family's financial situation made it difficult for her to begin her dance studies, but once she started, it was only a few months before she moved up en pointe and became a young prodigy. She played a lead role in *The Nutcracker* just eight months after starting ballet, and was performing on a professional level shortly after that. This was absolutely unheard of amongst classical dancers, as many ballerinas spend their whole lives training to reach that point. She drew lots of media attention and quickly became a prominent figure in ballet.

> **"The path to your success is not as fixed and inflexible as you think."**
>
> **—Misty Copeland**

SELENA: TEJANO ICON

Selena Quintanilla-Pérez was a famous Mexican American singer. She started at a very young age with her family in the group Selena y Los Dinos before going on to be a solo act. She faced criticism early on for her Tejano music, as the genre was male-dominated. Critics quickly changed their tune, however, and Selena became known as the "Queen of Tejano." Despite her short life, Selena remains one of the bestselling female Latin artists.

> **"The goal isn't to live forever, but to create something that will…"**
>
> **—Selena**

SHIRLEY TEMPLE: FROM CHILD ACTRESS TO GLOBAL AMBASSADOR

Shirley Temple, most easily recognized for her golden corkscrew curls, began working as a child actress since she was three years old. Born in California in 1928, she was discovered by a film corporation while at her dance school. Educational Films Corporation contracted her to perform in all-kid comedy films that parodied adult roles and recent events. She rose to fame after her appearance in *Bright Eyes,* and from there she continued to star in hit films that made her the number one box office draw in all of Hollywood. Her wholesome image brought a dose of happiness to Americans during the Great Depression. Following her highly successful career as a child actress, she became a diplomat and ambassador for the United States.

"Be brave and clear. Follow your heart and don't be overly influenced by outside factors. Be true to yourself."

—Shirley Temple

AUDREY HEPBURN: ELEGANCE NEVER LOOKED SO GOOD

Audrey was born in Ixelles, Brussels, but she spent most of her childhood in England, Belgium, and Amsterdam. After studying ballet with Sonia Gaskell in Amsterdam, she moved to London and began performing in West End theatrical productions as a chorus girl. She soon after started picking up minor appearances in films, however, it wasn't until Audrey starred in the Broadway production of *Gigi* that her career really started to take flight. After her appearance in *Gigi,* she landed the lead role in the film *Roman Holiday* and her career was never the same! She became a household name and a young girl that everyone wanted to both be and look like! Audrey set a whole new standard for fashion as Holly Golightly in *Breakfast at Tiffany's.* She soon became a fashion icon for decades to follow. She is also one of only a few actresses to earn EGOT status, wining an Emmy, a Grammy, an Oscar, and a Tony.

"Nothing is impossible, the word itself says, 'I'm Possible.' "
—Audrey Hepburn

ANNIE OAKLEY: A SHARPSHOOTER

Annie Oakley was born Phoebe Ann Moss on August 13, 1860, in Darke County, Ohio. Her father passed away when she was six years old, and her mother was left with six children to support. To lighten the load off her mother, Annie moved in with the family of Superintendent Edington. She stayed at the county infirmary, which housed a number of individuals unable to care for themselves, including children and elderly folks. In exchange for education and a place to stay, Annie would help take care of the orphaned children. This is where Annie's lifelong compassion for children comes from. When she returned to her family at thirteen years old, Annie's mother had remarried. However, their finances were still poor, so Annie started using the old rifle her father had left them to hunt game and help feed her family. Annie started to become extremely successful at shooting, more than she thought would be. What started out to just help feed her family and help pay the mortgage eventually turned into a sport. She became known for her notable shooting skills and was invited to shoot against well-known marksmen when she was just fifteen years old. She became a performer of Buffalo Bill's Wild West show, making her an international star as she grew in fame to perform for important figures and royalty.

> "Aim at a high mark and you'll hit it. No, not the first time, nor the second time. Maybe not the third. But keep on aiming and keep on shooting for only practice will make you perfect."
>
> **—Annie Oakley**

STORM REID: TAKING THE WORLD BY STORM

Storm Reid's acting career began when she was three. A string of small roles eventually led to her film debut in 2013's *12 Years a Slave*. This performance was followed by an appearance in the superhero movie *Sleight,* and then her breakout: Disney's *A Wrinkle in Time.* She also made numerous appearances on television, including *NCIS: Los Angeles* and *Chicago P.D.* She currently plays roles on the HBO series *Euphoria* and the Netflix series *Central Park.* In an interview with *The Washington Post* she said that her main goal was to "represent girls who look like me and let them know they can do anything."

> **"I'm gonna take this world by storm. Pun intended."**
> **—Storm Reid**

DARLA HOOD: THE LITTLE RASCAL

Darla was an American child actress who played the lead role in the *Little Rascals*. Darla got her love for the arts from her mother who taught her appreciation and skill for singing and dancing. Her career finally took off when she made her debut, unplanned, at the Edison Hotel in Times Square. The leader of the band invited her onto the stage, where she received an exuberant reaction from the audience. Luckily for Darla, agent Joe Rivkin happened to be in the audience that same night. He witnessed her performance and quickly signed a long-term contract with her. Her pay was $75 weekly, which is equal to $27,375 today. Because Darla went onstage that night, she is now one of the youngest actresses, and we should learn from Darla's serendipitous big break that every moment is an opportunity!

> "Take my heart, but please don't break it."
> —Darla Hood

AUBREY ANDERSON EMMONS: A MODERN ROLE MODEL

Aubrey is a child actress who played young Lily Tucker-Pritchett on ABC's *Modern Family*. In the show, Lily, a Vietnamese-born child, is adopted by a gay couple in America. Her performance in the role earned Aubrey praise for bringing more diversity and cultural awareness onto the screen. When she was four, she and the rest of the *Modern Family cast* won the Screen Actors Guild Award for Outstanding Performance by a Cast (or Ensemble) in a Comedy Series. As part of the ensemble, she became the youngest person to ever win a SAG award. She currently spends much of her time doing charity work for a number of different organizations.

> **"No matter what it is you want to do in life, it's important to be yourself."**
> **—Aubrey Anderson Emmons**

MILEY CYRUS: A GIRL WHO CAN'T BE TAMED

Miley Cyrus was originally born Destiny Hope, but her parents would always call her "Smiley," which would later evolve into Miley. Her desire to be an actress began early as she sat on the side and watched her father Billy Ray Cyrus perform on the TV series *Doc,* and it wasn't long until she soon wanted to be in front of the camera and not on the side. When Miley finally started her acting career, it wasn't as easy as most people think. It was actually filled with rejection, more than she could count at times. However, Miley kept stepping up to the plate to try again. Finally, she landed the role as Hannah Montana on the Disney Channel show of the same name. Very quickly, she became a teen idol and household name. Since her television series on Disney, she has become a successful musician with three number one albums and has starred in a few feature films, such as *The Last Song.*

> **"When life puts you in a tough situation,**
> **don't say 'Why me,' say 'Try me.' "**
> **—Miley Cyrus**

CHAPTER TEN

YOUNG FEMINISTS: GIRL POWER IS THE BEST POWER

Women in the past have struggled for equal pay, the right to work, the right to vote, and the chance to be heard. Even now, women are paid eighty-five cents on the dollar—Black women and Latinx women are paid even less. There is still work to be done to affect positive change by and for women. Now, finally the microphone is being passed around and girls and young women are getting that chance to speak their minds. At a young age, these girls were never afraid to stand up for their beliefs and continue the fight for.

Fighting like a girl means being strong and deliberate and making your voice be heard no matter what. "Girl power" is a force to be reckoned with, so be prepared to witness an epic showdown.

FU YUANHUI: REFRESHINGLY HONEST

Fu Yuanhui is a bronze medalist Chinese competitive swimmer who specializes in the backstroke. However, she is most known for helping remove the taboo about menstrual cycles in sports. After not performing as well as she wanted to during a race, Fu explained that she had gotten her period the day before and it was making her particularly exhausted. Fu's candid honesty about her struggles during the race received tons of positive feedback. Fu inspired girls all over the world to be more open about their periods and hopes one day talking about periods will be just as casual as hearing about a pulled muscle in the athletic world.

"I used all of my mystic energy!"
—Fu Yuanhui

EMMA WATSON: A WIZARD IN FEMINISM

Emma Watson, the iconic actress who played Hermione in the Harry Potter films, has proven that she is a force to be reckoned with. Despite her success in films, she continued to pursue her college education at Brown University. In 2014, Emma was selected as a UN Women Goodwill Ambassador and gave a speech at UN Headquarters to launch her #HeForShe campaign. The intention behind #HeForShe is to encourage people of all genders to fight for gender equality, standing in solidarity with and empowering women, and actively fighting to end gender-based violence. Emma also has a feminist book club called "Our Shared Shelf" to help spread feminism and what she is learning about feminism. She also traveled to several under-developed countries, such as Bangladesh, Zambia, and Uruguay to promote women's education and women's participation in politics.

"If women are terrified to use the word [feminism], how on earth are men supposed to start using it?"
—Emma Watson

LILINAZ EVANS: CREATING A DIALOGUE

For as long as she could remember, Lili didn't like what she saw in the mirror. Sometimes her reflection even made her physically ill because she wasn't society's ideal standard of beauty. This encouraged her to create the Twitter Youth Feminist Army, a platform where women can discuss feminist ideas, thinking, and destroy beauty standards.

> **"...I finally feel comfortable in my own body, which is—quite an achievement for me..."**
> **—Lili Evans**

ROSE LYDDON: SHARING HER STRENGTH

After being attacked and assaulted in her classroom, Rose Lyddon has become an activist for women's rights and preventing assaults against women. With her friend Necati, she is using social media as a tool to spread ideas and messages that women can be successful too. She is currently planning on being an ambassador for Shape Your Culture, a project that helps adolescents develop a good outlook on body image.

> **"[Feminism] saved my life."**
> **—Rose Lyddon**

JINAN YOUNIS: SHE WON'T LET SOCIETY DEFINE HER

Jinan is a young girl who decided to start a feminist group to help girls feel loved, accepted, and acknowledged, regardless of their ethnicity, size, economic backgrounds, or other distinguishing personal traits. She was inspired to spearhead this venture after she and her friends were repeatedly called nasty, derogatory, and sexist names. Her inspiration also came from seeing how many girls in her school had eating disorders, suffered in emotionally abusive relationships, and felt strong-armed into sexual acts due to the pressures associated with their gender. She took a whole year off of school to legitimize this group in society, however, she would be confronted with many obstacles along the way. Many boys in her wider peer group lashed out against her feminist group. She was accused of "feeding girls [feminist] bullshit." However, the boys' backlash just encouraged more girls at her school to raise their opinions and voices.

"I'm really excited for the future of feminism."
—Jinan Younis

ARANYA JOHAR: WORDS ARE HER WEAPON

Aranya is a girl who is not afraid to speak her mind. She uses writing and poetry to help bring awareness to the inequality and injustices brought against women in India. She also uses her poetry to help confront beauty standards. She and Akshay Kumar helped bring spoken word poetry into Bollywood films. Aranya also uses the tag "Brown Girl" to bring more positive representation of brown people to mainstream media. Aranya is currently the curator of several poetry gigs, like Blind Poetry nights.

> **"Forget snow white, say hello to chocolate brown. I'll write my own fairytale."**
> **—Aranya Johar**

AMANDLA STENBERG: A VOICE FOR THE FUTURE

Amandla Stenberg's big break was her role as Rue in the film adaptation of *The Hunger Games*. Since then, she has become one of the most outspoken feminists of this generation. She has used the internet and her platform to share essays and promote intersectional feminism. However, it was her video that she made for a high school class called *Don't Cash Crop My Cornrows* that thrust her into the feminist limelight. In her video, she discusses the ignorance of cultural appropriation and Black female issues.

> "It's a tiny revolution to express yourself fully and be who you want to be, especially when systems tell you that you can't. I've realized how powerful it is for me to just discuss with young people and begin conversations."
>
> —Amandla Stenberg

AMANI AL-KHATAHTBEH: SHE WILL BE HEARD

Amani is the founder and editor-in-chief of MuslimGirl.net, an online blog aimed at reclaiming the Muslim narrative and combating stereotypes. She started this website when she was just a teenager in high school because she was tired of feeling the frustration of everyone speaking on her behalf. People always present Muslim women as oppressed and voiceless, which has led to a lot of misrepresentation and misinformation. However, Amani is trying to change that.

> **"I needed to decide that I wanted to be first. That I could be first. That I, too, deserve to be first."**
>
> **—Amani Al-Khatahtbeh**

CHAPTER ELEVEN

GIRLS WHO STOOD UP: USING THEIR COURAGE TO MAKE CHANGE

Across history, women have been oppressed and taught to be silent. However, all around the world many girls have fought to put an end to this injustice. By using the power of education, they seek to make their voices heard. Despite the danger that being in the opposition puts them in, they persevere in order to be the voice of change for their fellow women.

One girl really can change the world. These girls have been put in impossible situations, situations that would overwhelm most adults, and still not only did the right thing but started conversations and made history in doing so. The girls in this chapter are some of the bravest individuals in history and their strength and gut instincts are beyond words.

DARNELLA FRAZIER: RECORDING HISTORY

While taking her nine-year-old niece on what was meant to be a simple trip to Cup Foods, Darnella Frazier witnessed a man, George Floyd, begging for his life as he was forcibly held to the ground with a police officer's knee pressed against his neck. Darnella, who was seventeen at the time, pulled out her cellphone and recorded the incident. The now infamous video went viral and sparked a resurgence in the Black Lives Matter movement, leading to huge protests in cities across the US. Darnella recalls being terrified to get involved and feeling guilty for not doing more, even though her video served as a key piece of evidence in the trial of Derek Chauvin. Darnella was an instrumental figure in this trial, recalling the fear she felt while, along with the other bystanders, she yelled at all officers involved telling them to stop hurting George Floyd. Combined with her powerful statements at the trial, Darnella's video evidence was used to convict Derek Chauvin on three counts of murder and manslaughter. Darnella rightfully received the PEN America Award for Courage for her act of bravery and has been praised by senators, journalists, filmmakers, and President Joe Biden. Darnella is a prime example of not only an awesome girl, but a *strong* girl.

> "Although no amount of charges will bring back a loved one, justice was served and his murderer will pay the price. We did it."
>
> —Darnella Frazier

MALALAI JOYA: SHE WILL NOT BE SILENCED

Malalai Joya speaks out against the violence of the Taliban in Afghanistan, despite the danger it puts her in. She has received death threats for her words and currently migrates from safe house to safe house to continue her work. At a young age, her mother took her and her nine siblings to Iran as refugees and migrated from there to Pakistan. There, Malalai learned her love for literature and reading. She began reading everything she could touch, and at the young age of sixteen, the Organization for Promoting Afghan Women's Capabilities (OPAWC) approached her about helping to establish an underground school. She was smuggled back to Afghanistan and continued her passion for teaching without the Taliban's notice. She was never caught and was promoted to director. After the Taliban's retreat after the American invasion in the wake of the 9/11 attacks, warlords replaced them as oppressors. Anti-women laws forced Malalai to stop running clinics for poor women, yet she refused. She ran for parliament and won, calling out the country for letting criminals harass them. She was dispelled for speaking out yet continues to fight for the people of Afghanistan and their rights. Despite having throngs of criminals after her, she continues to be the voice of her fellow Afghan women.

> "...they will not kill my voice, because it will be the voice of all Afghan women. You can cut the flower, but you cannot stop the coming of spring."
>
> —Malalai Joya

MUZOON ALMELLEHAN: CARRYING THE WORLD ON HER BACK

Learning that you must leave everything behind is a tough hurdle to overcome in life. Muzoon was told she had to flee her home in Syria when she was fourteen years old, and to only take what she could. She decided to fill her bag with books, knowing that even though it would be heavy to carry, it would be worth it to save her education. Living in the Jordanian refugee camps was difficult, but Muzoon let her passion for learning be a beacon of hope. The school in the camp was empty, and Muzoon found that it was due to all of the girls being married. She decided then and there to promote education and stand up for these girls' rights despite the fear in everyone's hearts and their attitudes toward arranged marriage. She worked to educate the girls' parents to let them study, and let education be a powerful tool. She was then approached by UNICEF and began to expand her crusade. Muzoon proves that circumstances do not have to dictate the future, and the power of one can spark a movement of change.

> **"If young people are not educated, who will rebuild our country?"**
> **—Muzoon Almellehan**

ZULAIKHA PATEL: A NATURAL BORN LEADER

School should be a place where all students are encouraged to learn and to be themselves. But for thirteen-year-old Zulaikha, school became a place where she felt marginalized. Pretoria's all-girls high school in South Africa, where Zulaikha attended, had a strict dress code policy that affected girls of color. Teachers told Zulaikha to "tame" her afro, and that her hair was unnatural. This led Zulaikha and other classmates to speak out, and they protested. They refused to change their natural hair and stood outside the school in protest. Zulaikha and her fellow young activists refused to back down, even as security guards entered the scene, and the students shouted, "take us all" with their hands in the air. They refused to be silenced, and their courage sparked a movement around South Africa and the rest of the world. By demanding respect, Zulaikha has shown the world that institutional racism still persists, and that students in schools refuse to back down.

> **"It's important for people to stand up for what
> they believe in, and that's what I'm doing."**
> **—Zulaikha Patel**

SHAEERA KALLA: NEVER STOP FIGHTING

A student representative council president at Wits University, Shaeera always believed in the power of protest. In her term as president, Shaeera felt the unfair increase in school fees further marginalized the poor students. She organized a committee and the slogan "WitsFeesMustFall." Their aim was to "systematically shut the school down." The movement caused other universities to hold similar protests, and Shaeera was the flagship. She received backlash from the police and school boards, but that did not stop her. During one protest at the school, police officers intervened. Shaeera tried to negotiate with the police officers and calm the students down when a police officer shot her multiple times with rubber bullets. In the hospital, Shaeera recovered and was as vocal as ever. She shows that in the face of fear, staying strong can inspire others.

"I hope that one day...we will not have to utter the hopeless truth, 'no one has been held accountable.' "

—Shaeera Kalla

NUPOL KIAZOLU: PAGEANT QUEEN, STUDENT, ACTIVIST

Nupol Kiazolu is the president of Black Lives Matter Greater New York. She was also the CEO and founder of Vote2000 at only eighteen years old. At age twelve, outraged by the death of Trayvon Martin, she wore a hoodie to school in protest with the words "Do I look suspicious to you?" written on it. She faced threat of suspension from her school but refused to take it off, and instead went home, researched her First Amendment rights as a student, and returned to make her argument to the school principal. He was convinced and let her wear it, inspiring a majority of the school to do the same. She aims to inspire Black youth, especially girls, to be active and stand up for themselves. Despite the constant danger of violence, Nupol consistently stands in the front lines during protests. She has and will continue to be an advocate for Black lives and youth.

"So with me using my voice to stand up for what's right and for social justice, it's really been critical, and there's young people like me doing the work everywhere."

—Nupol Kiazolu

ZIANNA OLIPHANT: A YOUNG ADVOCATE WITH A LOT TO SAY

Zianna Oliphant recently gave an emotional speech at the Charlotte City Council in anger and protest against violence in her community. At just nine years old, she was able to bring attention to police brutality as well as the Black Lives Matter movement on a national level. Her mother explained that her speech was unplanned, and the emotions that Zianna evoked were due to her passion for equality.

> **"We are Black people and we shouldn't have to feel like this. We shouldn't have to protest because y'all are treating us wrong."**
> **—Zianna Oliphant**

MAYA MOORE: A TRUE BALLER

Maya Moore is a professional basketball player superstar turned reformer. She sat out this past season, and will continue to sit out, in order to focus on a passion other than the game: criminal justice reform. After hearing about the case of Jonathan Irons, a man she believed to be wrongfully accused, she decided to work with him in order to learn about and push for change. While her dominating presence is missed in the WNBA and team USA, her decision is supported and understood. She participates in interviews and panels about her goal to see the prison system reformed, especially regarding its treatment of minorities. Moore has shifted from a playmaker to a change-maker.

"I'm here because I care."
—Maya Moore

MEENA KUMAR: NO PUP LEFT BEHIND

At the age of nine months, Meena Kumar was abandoned by her birth parents in Pune, India. She remained in an orphanage for about a year, before being adopted by a couple in Mumbai and moving to San Jose, California. She was fascinated by and loved to visit Muttville, a cage-free organization which aims to give senior dogs a "second chance at life." She wanted to volunteer but was too young. At age twelve, she decided to start her own business, "Pet Fairy Services," as a way to support Muttville. As of the time of writing, at just fourteen years old, she has raised $14,000. Meena knows what it is like to be abandoned and wants to give older dogs the second chance that she was given.

> "I think all dogs are really sweet and older dogs give the same unconditional love as other dogs and they should find a home because they've given so much."
>
> —Meena Kumar

MEGHAN SENEY: "EGG"-CELLENT ENTREPRENEUR

Meghan Seney is a nine-year-old owner of a business called MegsEggs, where she sells eggs to people in her community. While being that young of an entrepreneur is impressive, what makes Meghan awesome is her generous heart. As the pandemic swept the world, healthcare workers quickly realized that masks were a necessity that was becoming sparse. Meghan took her love for sewing and turned it into something that helped others. She began to sew masks for healthcare workers, friends, and family. As of May, she has sewn over 600 masks!

> **"There's so much good that can come out of giving to others."**
> **—Meghan Seney**

SABA ISMAIL: GIRLS HELPING GIRLS

Saba is a feminist and activist. At only fifteen years old, she co-founded "Aware Girls," an organization run by young women aiming to empower girls to fight for social change and take part in leadership opportunities. Due to her work and excellence on youth development and the prevention of violent extremism, the UN General Secretary appointed her to the Advisory Group for the Progress Study on Youth, Peace, and Security. To be so young yet to understand the importance of fighting for social change is what inspires others to follow in Saba's lead, and demand equal opportunities for girls and women globally.

> **"You have to take a step if you want to bring a change, and you have to do something."**
> **—Saba Ismail**

ILEANA CRUDU: SHE'S GOT THE IT FACTOR

Before graduating High School, Ileana entered into a program called GirlsGoIT, which is an inspirational program in Moldova (where Ileana is from) that empowers girls to break from traditional gender norms and teaches them valuable skills to enter into the IT field. After completing the program and graduating from high school, Ileana went on to study knowledge engineering at Maastricht University in the Netherlands. She is now a relentless ambassador for the program and encourages other girls to break down norms and study technology and code.

"I am proud if people say that I code like a girl because I know I can rock the world with my code!"
—Ileana Crudu

AUTUMN PELTIER: PLANET PROTECTOR

Teenage activist Autumn is from Ontario's Wiikwemkoong First Nation. While she may not be fully grown yet, she is an important figure in Canada's indigenous water protection movement. She has spoken out in front of the United Nations to project her vision where everyone has access to fresh water. Her list of accomplishments is stacked at such a young age. At the Global Landscapes Forum, a knowledge-led platform dedicated to sustainable landscapes backed by the United Nations Environment Programme, she has addressed prominent, world-renowned guests. She has even called out Prime Minister Justin Trudeau at an Assembly of First Nations meeting for breaking promises for climate change. She has spread her message for climate change across the globe at hundreds of events and was nominated for the 2019 International Children's Peace Prize. She will continue to advocate for clean water and other environmental issues.

> "This is our future we're trying to protect and take care of, because it's being basically destroyed."
> —Autumn Peltier

SOPHIA PIERRE-ANTOINE: PUTTING IN THE WORK

Born in Haiti, Sophia was inspired by her mother and sister who both advocated for women's rights. She became involved in the Young Women's Christian Association in Haiti where she joined in helping young women have a safe haven from abuse. She studied sociology and gender studies at Stony Brook University. At Stony Brook, she was able to continue her advocacy by joining feminist clubs and leadership organizations while returning to Haiti during the summer to work directly with young girls on their rights. After school she became the program officer and grew the number of young girls from 80 to 180, teaching them leadership skills, self-esteem, and physical rights. Now, she is on the World YWCA's Global Advisory Council and is the board co-chair for FRIDA Feminist Fund.

"I think that a big part of being a feminist is to make sure that young women know that they have rights and that they have bodily autonomy; that they can say no."

—Sophia Pierre-Antoine

TRISHA PRABHU: KEEPING KIDS SAFE ONLINE

Sometimes empathy and compassion can be a vehicle for change. At age twelve, Trisha was heartbroken when she read the news of Rebecca Sedwick, a thirteen-year-old who took her own life after years of cyberbullying. Having been a victim of online bullying and harassment herself, Trisha knew that something had to be done. She developed and patented "ReThink," a technology that detects and prevents cyberbullying at the source by changing minds before posting a hateful message. ReThink's success has been noted on a global platform and was featured on the TV show *Shark Tank*. In 2016, she was invited by Barack Obama to the Global Entrepreneurship Summit and was the first freshman to win the President Innovation Grand Prize from Harvard University, where she is currently attending.

> **"I knew I'd stumbled onto a world-changing idea—and ReThink was born."**
>
> **—Trisha Prabhu**

THANDIWE ABDULLAH: BLACK LIVES MATTER

Thandiwe Abdullah co-founded the Black Lives Matter Youth Vanguard and is also a Black Lives Matter organizer. She showed that passion can come from any age when, at fifteen, she launched the Black Lives Matter in Schools campaign. As a student herself, Abdullah wants to create a safe place for people of color and encourage them to rally against anti-Blackness. At an early age, Abdullah understood that activism was important, which did not make her popular amongst her peers. Regardless, she stood up to her classmates and even her teachers and held them accountable for their words and actions.

> **"The world we know right now is not something that we have to just sit back and accept."**
> **—Thandiwe Abdullah**

ESTELLA JUAREZ: MILITARY DAUGHTER WITH A CAUSE

Unfortunately, heartbreak does not escape the young and innocent. Estella Juarez was just nine years old when her immigrant mother was deported to Mexico. Her father, a member of the United States military who served in Iraq, voted for President Trump in 2016, believing that he would "protect military families." Estella was asked to speak at the 2020 Democratic National Convention at age eleven, and read a letter addressed to President Trump. In the letter, she claimed that her father would not vote for Donald Trump this term. Also, in her heartbreaking letter, she voiced the pain that many families have felt as their family was torn apart. She articulately described that these people are not "animals" and that children should not be held in cages. Estella proves that even the youngest of us can have a strong voice and make a difference.

"We are American families. We need a president who will bring people together, not tear them apart."
—Estella Juarez

CONCLUSION

If the brave and inspiring girls in this book have taught you anything, it should be that you can *literally* do anything you put your mind to. These girls have shown time and time again that it is not your gender or your age that decides your capability; it is your inner strength and confidence that proves just how capable you are of doing incredible things. Girls have been proving their leadership skills and aptitude for years and years. They have been making history and kicking ass since humankind began to as recently as yesterday. My hope is that these fierce young women remind you that you are made up of the same magic as they are, and you can share that magic just as they did (and continue to do). My one request to you is this: never stop believing in yourself and the girls around you. You all have an innate power inside of you, and I know you will use that power to not only lift up yourself, but others around you as well. Take the lessons you have learned from this book and bring them into your everyday life. When someone says, "No," you say, "Alright, but I'm gonna do it anyway." When someone says, "You're too young," you say, "Age is nothing only a number." And if someone ever tells you that you cannot do something because you are a girl, I know you will stand tall, look them straight in the eyes and say, "Yes, I am a girl and that is exactly why I *can* do this." Never forget: You. Are. Awesome. Now go out and change the world!

WHO ARE YOUR AWESOME GIRLS?

Dear Reader,

This book almost never made it to the printer because we kept finding more and more fascinating girls deserving to be honored in the archives of history. We would love to have a follow-up volume detailing the lives and times of more role models. We invite you to email, Tweet, DM, or send a note with your nomination of your Awesome Girl. We would love to hear from you about this and continue the celebration of the "great unknowns" who didn't make it into the history books, UNTIL NOW!

Below is a simple nomination form, and we would love to credit you, so please include your contact information. Thanks for your participation—you are pretty awesome yourself!

XOXO
Becca

- -

I Nominate the Following Awesome Girls:

_____

_____

_____

_____

_____

Mango Publishing 2850 Douglas Road
2nd Floor Coral Gables, Florida 33134
Twitter: @MangoPublishing Email info@Mango.bz

ABOUT THE AUTHOR

Becca Anderson comes from a long line of preachers and teachers from Ohio and Kentucky. The teacher side of her family led her to become a woman's studies scholar and the author of *The Book of Awesome Women*. An avid collector of meditations, prayers and blessings, she helps run a "Gratitude and Grace Circle" that meets monthly at homes, churches and bookstores in the San Francisco Bay Area where she currently resides. Becca Anderson credits her spiritual practice with helping her recover from cancer and wants to share this with anyone who is facing difficulty in their life.

Author of *Think Happy to Stay Happy* and *Every Day Thankful*, Becca Anderson shares her inspirational writings and suggested acts of kindness at:
https://thedailyinspoblog.wordpress.com/

She also blogs about Awesome Women at:
https://theblogofawesomewomen.wordpress.com/

Mango Publishing, established in 2014, publishes an eclectic list of books by diverse authors—both new and established voices—on topics ranging from business, personal growth, women's empowerment, LGBTQ studies, health, and spirituality to history, popular culture, time management, decluttering, lifestyle, mental wellness, aging, and sustainable living. We were recently named 2019 *and* 2020's #1 fastest-growing independent publisher by *Publishers Weekly.* Our success is driven by our main goal, which is to publish high quality books that will entertain readers as well as make a positive difference in their lives.

Our readers are our most important resource; we value your input, suggestions, and ideas. We'd love to hear from you—after all, we are publishing books for you!

Please stay in touch with us and follow us at:

Facebook: Mango Publishing
Twitter: @MangoPublishing
Instagram: @MangoPublishing
LinkedIn: Mango Publishing
Pinterest: Mango Publishing
Newsletter: mangopublishinggroup.com/newsletter

Join us on Mango's journey to reinvent publishing, one book at a time.